SHED: EXPLODED VIEW

by Phoebe Eclair-Powell

Shed: Exploded View was first performed at
the Royal Exchange Theatre, Manchester
on 9 February 2024.

SHED: EXPLODED VIEW
by Phoebe Eclair-Powell

Lil	Hayley Carmichael
Frank	Jason Hughes
Abi	Norah Lopez Holden
Tony	Wil Johnson
Naomi	Lizzy Watts
Mark	Michael Workéyè

Director	Atri Banerjee
Designer	Naomi Dawson
Lighting Designer	Bethany Gupwell
Sound Designer	Max Pappenheim
Composer	Carmel Smickersgill
Movement Director	Sung Im Her
Voice and Dialect Coach	Natalie Grady
Production Dramatherapist	Wabriya King
Casting Director	Nadine Rennie CDG
Birkbeck Assistant Director	Amara Heyland

Dramaturg	Suzanne Bell
Bruntwood Coordinator	Rosie Thackeray

Production Manager	Hannah Blamire for The Production Family

Stage Manager	Sophie Wright
Deputy Stage Manager	Amy Bending
Interim Deputy Stage Manager	Natasha Guzel
Assistant Stage Manager	Amelia Blackburn

Hayley Carmichael (Lil)

Theatre credits include: *The Killing of Sister George* (The New Vic); *Super High Resolution* (Soho Theatre); *Home* (Chichester Festival Theatre); *Why/The Prisoner* (Peter Brook/Théâtre des Bouffes du Nord); *Beyond Caring* (The Yard); *Too Clever By Half* (Royal Exchange Theatre/Told By An Idiot); *Hamlet* (Young Vic); *Forests* (Birmingham Rep/Barbican); *Sweet Nothings* (Young Vic); *Bliss* (Royal Court); *Casanova* (Told By An Idiot/Leeds Playhouse); *The Maids* (Brighton Festival); *Cymbeline* (Kneehigh); *Zumanity* (Cirque du Soleil); *Theatre of Blood* (Improbable/National Theatre); *Street of Crocodiles* (Complicité/National Theatre). Television credits include: *Silent Witness*, *Les Misérables* (BBC); *Landscapers* (HBO); *Witness for the Prosecution* (Mammoth Screen); *Kiss Me First* (Balloon); *Our Zoo* (Big Talk Productions). Film credits include: *Casanova/Le Dernier Amour* (Bluelight); *Underdogs* (Vennerfilm); *Tale of Tales* (Archimede); *Tonight the World/A Hunger Artist* (Daria Martin).

Jason Hughes (Frank)

Trained at LAMDA. Theatre credits include: *To Kill a Mockingbird* (Gielgud Theatre); *Our Country's Good*, *Look Back in Anger* (National Theatre); *Way Upstream* (Chichester Festival Theatre); *On Bear Ridge*, *Violence and Son*, *4:48 Psychosis*, *A Real Classy Affair* (Royal Court); *Caligula*, *Badfinger* (Donmar Warehouse); *The Fight for Barbara*, *Design for Living* (Theatre Royal, Bath); *Kiss Me Like You Mean It* (Soho Theatre); *In Flame* (Ambassadors Theatre); *The Herbal Bed* (RSC); *Snake in the Grass* (Old Vic); *The Goat, Or Who Is Sylvia?* (Theatre Royal Haymarket); *The Illusion* (Royal Exchange Theatre); *In the Next Room (Or The Vibrator Play)* (St James Theatre). Television credits include: *McDonald and Dodds*, *The Pact*, *Three Girls*, *This Life* & *This Life +10*, *Marcella*, *Midsomer Murders*, *Archer*, *King Girl*, *Pornography*, *Mine All Mine*, *Harry Enfield Yule Log Chums*. Film credits include: *Save the Cinema*, *Crow*, *Dead Long Enough*, *Dirty Bomb*, *Mabel*, *Phoenix Blue*, *Killing Me Softly*, *House*, *Shooters*, *Jimmy Fizz*.

Norah Lopez Holden (Abi)

Stage credits include: *The Flea* (The Yard Theatre); *The Art of Illusion* (Hampstead Theatre); *Hamlet* (Young Vic); *Equus* (Theatre Royal Stratford East); *The Winter's Tale/Eyam* (Shakespeare's Globe); *The Almighty Sometimes*, *Our Town* (Royal Exchange Theatre); *Ghosts* (HOME); *Epic Love and Pop Songs* (Pleasance Theatre). Radio credits include: *Our Friends in the North*, and various other productions for BBC Radio 4.

Wil Johnson (Tony)

Theatre acting credits include: *Jitney* (Old Vic); *Running with Lions* (Lyric Hammersmith); *Sweat* (Donmar Warehouse/Gielgud Theatre); *Rosencrantz & Guildenstern are Dead* (Old Vic); *King Lear* (Royal Exchange Theatre). Television credits include: *House of the Dragon* (HBO Max); *Cobra: Rebellion* (SKY); *Carnival Row* (Legendary Television); *Outlander* (Amazon); *Emmerdale* (ITV Yorkshire); *Waking the Dead* (BBC); *Clocking Off* (Red Productions). Film credits include: *Anuvahood* (Revolver); *Adulthood* (Adulthood Limited); *In A Better World* (Zentropa); *Babymother* (Channel 4/Formation Films Production).

Lizzy Watts (Naomi)

Theatre credits include: *Ravenscourt, Either* (Hampstead Theatre); *The False Servant, Dealing with Clair* (Orange Tree Theatre); *Hedda Gabler* (National Theatre); *Strife* (Chichester Festival Theatre); *The Angry Brigade* (Paines Plough/Bush Theatre); *God of Chaos and Merit* (Theatre Royal, Plymouth); *A Midsummer Night's Dream* (Shakespeare's Globe); *Blink* (Soho Theatre/NY); *Twelfth Night* (Filter Theatre); *Wasted* (Paines Plough); *Artefacts* (Nabokov/Bush Theatre). Television credits include: *Professor T; Call the Midwife; Endeavour; The Durrells.* Lizzy played Ivy Layton in Radio 4's *Homefront* and has been a member of the BBC's Radio Rep company twice, appearing in numerous radio productions.

Michael Workéyè (Mark)

Since graduating from Arts Educational drama school in 2019, Michael has starred in: *Sitting in Limbo* (BBC); *Big Age* (Channel 4); and the highly acclaimed BBC One drama series *This Is Going to Hurt* starring Ben Whishaw. He was nominated for a *Stage* Debut Award for Best Actor with his outstanding performance in *House of Ife* at the Bush Theatre in 2022. Last year Michael starred in *My Lady Jane*, an upcoming British television series made for Amazon Prime Video. Most recently he has filmed *Playdate* (Disney+).

Phoebe Eclair-Powell (Writer)

Phoebe Eclair-Powell is a writer from South East London. Her theatre credits include: *DORIAN* with Owen Horsley (Reading Rep, 2021); *Really Big and Really Loud* (Paines Plough, 2021); *HARM* (Bush Theatre, one of the *Guardian*'s top 10 plays of 2021); *The Picture of Dorian Gray* (Watermill Theatre 2018); *These Bridges* (National Theatre Connections Festival, 2018); *TORCH* with Jess Edwards (Underbelly, New Diorama, 2016); *Epic Love and Pop Songs* (Pleasance Theatre 2016); *FURY* (Soho Theatre, runner up for the Verity Bargate Award, 2016 winner of the Tony Craze Award); *WINK* (Theatre503, 2015, nominated for Best New Play, Offies). Her recent TV credits include: *The Road Trip* (ep 3 and 4, Paramount +); *HARM* (BBC 4); *Two Weeks to Live* (Sky); *Hollyoaks* (Channel 4). Phoebe has also been involved with the writers room for several shows including: *Tin Star* (Sky); *Letter to the King* (Netflix); *Gauntlet* (Sky) and *Domino Day* (BBC Three).

Atri Banerjee (Director)

Trained at Birkbeck, on the National Theatre Directors' Course, and as Trainee Director at the Royal Exchange Theatre. His previous directing credits for the Royal Exchange include *The Glass Menagerie, Hobson's Choice* (winner Best Director *The Stage* Debut Awards 2019) and *Utopia.* Other theatre directing credits include: *Julius Caesar* (RSC); *Britannicus* (Lyric Hammersmith); *Kes* (Octagon Theatre Bolton/Theatre by the Lake); *HARM* (Bush Theatre); *ERROR ERROR ERROR* (Marlowe Theatre/RSC); *Into the Woods* (BOVTS); *Europe* (LAMDA). Film directing credits include: *HARM* (BBC/Angelica Films/Bush Theatre). Atri is a recipient of the Peter Hall Bursary at the National Theatre, Creative Associate at the Gate Theatre, a Trustee of the Regional Theatre Young Directors' Scheme (RTYDS), and formerly a Resident Director at the Almeida Theatre.

Naomi Dawson (Designer)

Trained at Wimbledon School of Art and Kunstacademie, Maastricht. Previous designs for the Royal Exchange Theatre: *Light Falls*, *Happy Days*. Other work includes: *Hope has a Happy Meal*, *That Is Not Who I Am/Rapture*, *Scenes with Girls*, *The Woods* (Royal Court); *The Breach*, *The Animal Kingdom*, *Akedah*, *Belongings*, *Wildefire*, *The Gods Weep* (Hampstead Theatre); *Fair Play* (Bush Theatre); *Romeo and Juliet*, *As You Like It* (Regent's Park); *Twelfth Night* (Guthrie Theater, US); *The Convert*, *The Container* (Young Vic); *The Duchess of Malfi*, *Doctor Faustus*, *The White Devil*, *The Roaring Girl*, *As You Like It*, *King John* (RSC); *The Tin Drum* (Kneehigh); *The Winter's Tale* (Romateatern, Sweden); *Beryl* (Leeds Playhouse/UK tour); *Kasimir and Karoline*, *Fanny and Alexander* (Malmö Stadsteater, Sweden); *Brave New World* (Royal & Derngate, Northampton/UK tour); *Hotel*, *Three More Sleepless Nights* (National Theatre).

Bethany Gupwell (Lighting Designer)

Studied Lighting Design at the Royal Central School of Speech and Drama. She was winner of the Association of Lighting Designers' Francis Reid Award 2018 and nominated for Best Lighting Design Offies for *This Much I Know* (Hampstead Theatre, 2023); *A-Typical Rainbow* (Turbine Theatre, 2022); *Queen of the Mist* (Charing Cross Theatre, 2019). Recent credits include: *The Earthworks* (Young Vic); *This Much I Know*, *To Have and To Hold* (Hampstead Theatre); *A Play for the Living in a Time of Extinction*, *Lay Down Your Burdens* (Barbican); *La Voix Humaine* (Opéra National du Rhin); *A Rice, Little Baby Jesus* (Orange Tree Theatre); *Wickies*, *When Darkness Falls* (Park 200); *Here*, *The Woods* (Southwark Playhouse); *Talking Heads* (Watford Palace); *You Heard Me*, *Trade* (UK tour); *Brown Girls Do It Too: Mama Told Me Not To Come*, *Fitter*, *Wonder Winterland* (Soho Theatre); *War & Culture*, *little scratch*, *Keep Watching* (New Diorama Theatre); *Ignition* (Frantic Assembly); *The Pirate, The Princess and the Platypus* (Polka Theatre); *The Last Harvest* (National Youth Theatre).

Max Pappenheim (Sound Designer)

Theatre credits include: *The Night of the Iguana*, *Cruise* (West End); *A Doll's House Part 2*, *The Way of the World* (Donmar Warehouse); *Henry V* (Shakespeare's Globe); *Village Idiot*, *One Night in Miami* (Nottingham Playhouse); *Anthropology*, *Blackout Songs*, *Sea Creatures* (Hampstead Theatre); *Hamlet* (Bristol Old Vic/BBC Four); *The Children* (Royal Court/Broadway); *Feeling Afraid As If Something Terrible Is Going To Happen*, *Old Bridge* (Bush Theatre); *Ophelias Zimmer* (Royal Court/Schaubühne). Opera and ballet credits include: *The Marriage of Figaro* (Salzburg Festival); *Miranda* (Opéra Comique, Paris); *Hansel and Gretel* (BYO/Opera Holland Park); *Scraww* (Trebah Gardens); *Carmen: Remastered* (ROH/Barbican). Radio credits include: *Home Front* (BBC Radio 4). Awards include the Off West End Award for Sound Design (*Old Bridge*). Associate Artist of The Faction and Silent Opera.

Carmel Smickersgill (Composer)

Carmel Smickersgill is a Manchester-based composer and performer. She studied composition at the RNCM with Gary Carpenter. After which, she received the Rushworth Composition Prize with the Liverpool Philharmonic. She has since written for classical ensembles such as Manchester Camerata, BCMG and Ensemble 10/10. She has previously been an Ivor Novello Rising Star nominee. In 2022 she released her debut EP with PRAH recordings, under the mentorship of Anna Meredith who Carmel has been a support act for multiple times. Carmel first moved into theatre with Liz Richardson's production *Swim* (2018/2022), since then she has worked with companies ThisEgg and YESYESNONO including the score for *We Were Promised Honey!* (2022), which was a 2023 multiple Offie Award nominee.

Sung Im Her (Movement Director)

Sung Im Her is from Seoul, South Korea and obtained a master's degree in contemporary dance at Hansung University. In 2004, she moved to Brussels, Belgium to study at P.A.R.T.S., the contemporary dance school led by Anne Teresa De Keersmaeker/ROSAS. After graduating in 2006, she started working with Jan Fabre/Troubleyn, Les ballets C de la B and Needcompany in Belgium. In parallel Sung Im Her has been creating works of her own, starting with *Philia* (2012); *En-trance* (2013); *Tuning* (2014) and *You Are Okay!* (2016). In 2019, with *Nutcrusher* she was elected by the Korean Arts Council as Best Emerging Artist of 2019. *Nutcrusher* was also selected for Aerowaves Twenty21 and in 2022 it was a part of Horizon showcase, presented during the Edinburgh Fringe Festival where she received five-star reviews. Last year, Sung Im created *Everything Falls Dramatic* for Korean National Contemporary Dance Company which toured in Seoul, Madrid, Brussels, Manchester and London. The show received Dance Artist of the year in 2022 by the Korean Ministry of Culture and was recently named one of ten stage sensations to watch out for in 2023 by the *Guardian*.

Natalie Grady (Voice and Dialect Coach)

TV and film credits include: *One Day*, *Fool Me Once* (Netflix); *The Lazarus Project* (SKY); *Time* (series 1 and 2; BBC); *Boat Story* (C4); *Better* (BBC); *Happy Valley* (BBC); *The Reckoning* (BBC); *Your Christmas Or Mine* (Amazon); *The Gallows Pole* (BBC); *Somewhere Boy* (C4); *Red Rose* (NETFLIX); *McDonald and Dodds* (ITV); *Rules of the Game* (BBC); *Annie* (ITV); *Jingle Bell Christmas* (Hallmark); *Wolfe* (SKY); *Stephen* (ITV); *The Ipcress File* (ITV); *Ackley Bridge* (C4); *All Creatures Great And Small* (C5 and PBS for the US); *The Cure* (Channel 4); *Gwen* (Endor Productions). Theatre credits include: for the Royal Exchange: *Cat On A Hot Tin Roof*, *The Glass Menagerie*, *Nora: A Doll's House*, *Glee and Me*, *Wuthering Heights*, *Gypsy*, *Light Falls*, *West Side Story*, *Queens of the Coal Age*. Other credits include: *Hangmen* (Broadway); *To Kill A Mockingbird* (UK tour and Barbican) and various productions at Sheffield Crucible, Storyhouse, Bolton Octagon, Oldham Colliseum, Hull Truck, Theatre Clwyd, Theatre by the Lake, Stephen Joseph, RNCM, British Youth Opera.

Wabriya King (Production Dramatherapist)

Wabriya King is a qualified dramatherapist (Roehampton University), actress (The Oxford School of Drama), creative facilitator and Reiki practitioner. Wabriya combines her experience to support creatives alongside the rehearsal and performance period. Dramatherapy support credits include: *Beautiful Thing, Tambo & Bones* (Theatre Royal Stratford East); *A Strange Loop* (Barbican); *Cowbois, Falkland Sound, The Empress, Julius Caesar* (RSC); *School Girls, Or, The African Mean Girls Play* (Lyric Hammersmith); Matthew Bourne's *Romeo and Juliet* (New Adventures); *Drive Your Plow Over the Bones of the Dead* (Complicité); *Romeo and Juliet, Secret Life of Bees* (Almeida Theatre); *August in England* (Bush Theatre); *For Black Boys Who Have Considered Suicide When The Hue Gets Too Heavy* (New Diorama Theatre/Royal Court/West End); *Blue* (ENO); *Further than the Furthest Thing* (Young Vic); *Family Tree* (Actors Touring Company); *Bootycandy* (Gate Theatre); *Blues for an Alabama Sky* (National Theatre); *Hamilton, Moulin Rouge* (West End).

Nadine Rennie CDG (Casting Director)

Nadine Rennie has over twenty years' experience as a casting director for theatre. She was in-house Casting Director at Soho Theatre for fifteen years; working on new plays by writers including Dennis Kelly, Bryony Lavery, Arinzé Kene, Roy Williams, Philip Ridley, Laura Wade, Hassan Abdulrazzak, Phoebe Waller-Bridge and Oladipo Agboluaje. Since going freelance in January 2019 Nadine has worked for theatres and companies across London and the UK, including Arcola Theatre, Orange Tree Theatre, Leeds Playhouse, Paines Plough, Fuel Theatre, National Theatre of Wales, Northern Stage, Wildcard, Wales Millennium Centre, Kiln Theatre, Park Theatre, Theatre503, HOME Manchester, Pleasance Theatre London, Almeida, Lyric Hammersmith, Hampstead and Minack Theatres. She continues to cast on a regular basis for Soho Theatre and has a long running relationship with Synergy Theatre Project as their Casting Director/Consultant. TV work includes BAFTA-winning CBBC series *Dixi*, casting the first three series. Nadine is a member of the Casting Directors Guild and currently sits on the Committee.

Amara Heyland (Birkbeck Assistant Director)

Amara Heyland is training at Birkbeck University on the MFA Theatre Directing. She is a visiting director and facilitator at Rose Bruford College and is the Resident Assistant Director at the Royal Exchange Theatre, 2022–24. Credits as Director include: *Corpselight* (Masterclass Pitch Your Play Winner 2023, The Other Palace Theatre); *Blackthorn* (Bread and Roses Theatre, Drayton Arms Theatre, Etcetera Theatre); *Paper Boats* (Town & Gown Theatre); *The Dazzle* (Corpus Playroom). Credits as Assistant and Associate Director include: *Brief Encounter, Great Expectations* (Royal Exchange Theatre); *truth and reconciliation* (Rose Bruford College); *The Jazz Section* (The Union Theatre/Camden Fringe); *A Midsummer Night's Dream* (The Space @ Soulton Hall); *Mary Stuart* (Cambridge Round Church).

Manchester's Royal Exchange Theatre company transforms the way people see theatre, each other and the world around them. Our historic building was taken over by artists in 1976. Today it is an award-winning cultural charity that produces new theatre in-the-round, in communities, on the road and online.

Exchange remains at the heart of everything we make and do. Now our currency is brand new drama and reinvigorated classics, the boldest artists and a company of highly skilled makers – all brought together in a shared imaginative endeavour to trade ideas and experiences with the people of Greater Manchester (and beyond).

The Exchange's unique auditorium is powerfully democratic, a space where audiences and performers meet as equals, entering and exiting through the same doors. It is the inspiration for all we do; inviting everyone to understand the past, engage in today's big questions, collectively imagine a better future and lose themselves in the moment of a great night out.

The Royal Exchange was named Regional Theatre of the Year in 2016 and School of the Year at The Stage Awards 2018. Our work, developed with an incredible array of artists and theatre makers, includes the World Premiere of *untitled f*ck m*ss s**gon play* (Roy Alexander Weise), written by 2019 International Bruntwood Prize winner Kimber Lee and in collaboration with Manchester International Festival, the Young Vic and Headlong, *Hamlet* with Maxine Peake (for stage and film), *The Skriker* (with the Manchester International Festival), *Betty! A Sort Of Musical*, *Our Town*, *Light Falls* (a world-premiere from Simon Stephens with original music by Jarvis Cocker) all directed by Sarah Frankcom. *King Lear* (co-produced with Talawa Theatre Company, filmed for BBC iPlayer and BBC Four), *The House of Bernarda Alba* (a co-production with Graeae Theatre Company), *Rockets and Blue Lights* (by award-winning writer Winsome Pinnock and directed by Miranda Cromwell), *The Producers* (Raz Shaw) and *Beginning*, *Let The Right One In* and *No Pay? No Way!* (Bryony Shanahan).

royalexchange.co.uk

FOR THE ROYAL EXCHANGE

EXECUTIVE TEAM
Steve Freeman
Gina Fletcher

ENGAGEMENT
Andy Barry
Sam Holland-Bunyan
Katrina Heath
Inga Hirst
Sadia Mir
Ruvarashe Nyakupinda
Emily Oldroyd
Ria Phatarphekar
Scarlett Spiro-Beazley
Tom Stocks
Molly Taylor

MARKETING
Dhanna Estinozo
Fallon Mayne
Paula Rabbitt
Liam Steers
Morayo Sodipo
Vicky Wormald

DEVELOPMENT
Rosie Bingham
Rachel Morris

CREATIVE
Suzanne Bell
Rosie Thackeray
Nickie Miles-Wildin

THE RIVALS
Laurie Bailey-Higgins
Mark Beattie
Grace Bennett
Neve Clark
Leah Curran
Tatana Dubjukova
Romania Duffy
Lewis Eades
Martha Edwards
Theresa Fortune
Jess Gale
Matt Gunn
Amara Heyland
Kate Ireland
Hasan Isingor
Sedgwick James
Zofia Komorowska
Calima Lunt
Lois Mackie
Oonagh Maclennan
Lola Middleton
Ashley O'Brien
Jay Ottewell
Carolyn Pickering
Daniel Plews
Beata Potrzebouska
Kacper Potrzebouska
Anna Pullar
Jake Rayner Blair
Julie Rogers
Ethan Rudd
Rebecca Sharples
Gareth Smith
Helen Thomason
Lydia Trench
Rachel Zanetti

OPERATIONS
Matt Averall
Caitlin Conners
Rachel Davies
Frank Hill
Ashley Foster
Chris Owen
Mike Seal
Christiaan De Villiers

HR
Michelle Hickman
Yvonne Cox

VISITOR EXPERIENCE ASSISTANTS
Vicky Absolon, Richard Barry, Verity Bate, Anusia Battersby, Katy Brooks, Laura Brunk, Clodagh Chapman, Mika Cholewa, Aimee Clark, Amelia Cox, Molly Crighton, Tsen Day-Beaver, Céline Laissardière, Liam Dodd, Martha Edwards, Rosa Gatley, Neil Geddes, Connie Hartley, Ioana Hayder, Katrina Heath, Emma Hill, Jenny Hill, Olivia Holder, Maisie Holland, Max Holmes, Jennifer Hulman, Vistie James, Megan Jones, Josie Julyan, Waleria Koba, Connie Lane, Debbie Leech, Benjamin Lucas, Calima Lunt, Ronan Mcgrath, Alistair Mcnicol, Katie Merrick, Tony O'Driscoll, Chris Owen, Saskia Pay, Xsara Sheneille Pryce, Anna Pullar, Adam Rogers, Julia Rogers, Noor Shahid, Ayshea Shames, Holly Simpson, Tilly Sutcliffe, Helen Thomason, Che Tligui, Caitlyn Vining, Matthew Warren, Eliott Whittle, Mahdi Zadeh

VISITOR EXPERIENCE COORDINATORS
Amelia Cox, Liam Dodd, Maisie Holland, Vistie James, Ronan McGrath, Katie Merrick, Anna Pullar, Molly Crighton, Clodagh Chapman

CASUAL DUTY MANAGERS
Daniel Hird, Vistie James, Chris Owen

PRODUCING
Laura-Kate Ainsworth
Amy Chandler
Martha Ford Tomlinson
Richard Morgan
Anna Mountry
Scott McDonald

PRODUCTION
Grace Bastyan
Mark Distin Webster
Tracy Dunk
Bridget Fell
Louis Fryman
Amara Heyland
Felicia Jagne
Matt Lever
Owen Lewis
Alex Malinowski
Matt Masson
Connor Owens
Katerina Petmezas
Joanna Shepstone
Rachel Skelton
Tom Sutcliffe
Sarah White

FINANCE
James Howard
Vicii Kirkpatrick
Joanne Tasker

CLEANING CONTRACTORS
Mavis Asantewan, Sue Borough, Elaine Connolly, Linda Egbon, Moussa Kouyate, Ewa Opala, Solomon Onajnfe, Malgorzata Pagiela, Karolina Sawczuk

bruntwood

The Bruntwood Group includes Bruntwood and Bruntwood SciTech and is one of the UK's leading property providers, committed to creating thriving cities and town centres for over 47 years.

Bruntwood Group has over £1.7bn in assets and more than 100 properties across Greater Manchester, Cheshire, Leeds, Liverpool, Birmingham, Cambridge and Glasgow.

Bruntwood provides workspace, residential, retail and leisure space, including the independent shopping emporium, Afflecks in Manchester City Centre.

Focused on forming long-term, consultation-led partnerships to revitalise town centres, the business has a portfolio of town centre regeneration projects with Trafford and Bury Councils. Through a community-focussed approach to regeneration, Bruntwood aims to ensure social, economic and environmental sustainability and to create vibrant places that are dynamic, inspirational and futureproof.

Since 2018, Bruntwood has been a shareholder in Bruntwood SciTech alongside Legal & General, and was joined by Greater Manchester Pension Fund in October 2023. Bruntwood SciTech is the UK's leading developer of city-wide innovation ecosystems and specialist environments helping companies – particularly those in the science and technology sectors – to form, scale and grow. It is also the largest dedicated property platform serving the growth of the UK's knowledge economy to become a global science and technology superpower.

Recognising the urgency of the climate crisis, Bruntwood is also committed to a sustainable and fair future, and was the UK's first commercial property company to sign up to the UK Green Building Council's Advancing Net Zero Programme. By 2030, Bruntwood will operate at net zero carbon in the areas under its direct control and in the construction of new builds and major redevelopments, and will be a net zero business by 2050.

Bruntwood also actively collaborates with ambitious and ground-breaking arts and cultural organisations, in addition to supporting environmental, civic and charitable initiatives through the OCT.

bruntwood.co.uk

the bruntwood
prize for playwriting
in partnership with the **Royal Exchange Theatre**

A partnership between the Royal Exchange Theatre and property company Bruntwood, the Prize is an opportunity for writers of any background and experience to enter unperformed plays to be judged by a panel of industry experts.

Since its inception in 2005 over 15,000 scripts have been entered, £304,000 has been awarded to 34 prize-winning writers and 27 winning productions have been staged in 39 UK wide venues. At the heart of the Bruntwood Prize for Playwriting is the principle that anyone and everyone can enter the Prize – it is entirely anonymous and scripts are judged purely on the basis of the work alone and with no knowledge of the identity of the playwright.

Each winner enters into a development process with the Royal Exchange Theatre in an endeavour to bring their work to production. There have been co-productions with the Bush Theatre, Ellie Keel Productions, HighTide, Live Theatre, Lyric Hammersmith, Manchester International Festival, Mercury Theatre Colchester, Orange Tree Theatre, Paines Plough Theatre Company, Royal Court Theatre, Sherman Theatre, Soho Theatre, and the Young Vic Theatre. Work has also gone on to be produced internationally from Australia, Canada, France, Germany, Sweden and the USA.

The Bruntwood Prize International Award was launched in 2019 and, through partnerships with theatres and organisations in Australia, Canada and the US, accepts submissions from playwrights.

The Bruntwood Prize for Playwriting is a genuine endeavour to discover new stories and support playwrights to develop their craft, providing everybody and anybody with the opportunity to explore their creativity and write a play. It offers a fantastic opportunity to hone your writing skills whether or not you have written for the stage before.

More information can be found at **writeaplay.co.uk**

DONORS AND SUPPORTERS

PRINCIPAL FUNDERS

CORPORATE PARTNER
Bruntwood

CORPORATE SPONSOR
Edwardian Hotels
Galloways Printers
Garratts Solicitors
Stock Exchange Hotel
Verdure Floral Design
Warner Bros.Discovery

PRINCIPAL CORPORATE MEMBER
Edmundson Electrical

ENCORE CORPORATE MEMBER
Ralli Solicitors LLP
Slater Heelis

ASSOCIATE CORPORATE MEMBER
5plus Architects
Beaverbrooks the Jewellers Ltd
Sanderson Weatherall

TRUSTS AND FOUNDATIONS
The Backstage Trust
The Beaverbrooks Charitable Trust
The D'Oyly Carte Charitable Trust
The Esmée Fairbairn Foundation
The Granada Foundation
The Noël Coward Foundation
The Oglesby Charitable Trust
One Manchester & Manchester City Council
The Rayne Foundation
The Victoria Wood Foundation

RXIGNITE COLLECTIVE & SPECIAL ACKNOWLEDGEMENTS
Arnold & Brenda Bradshaw
The Baker Family Charitable Trust
Susan & Sally Hodgkiss CBE
Torevell & Partners

OUR TRAILBLAZERS
Jason Austin
Ben & Becky Caldwell
Meg & Peter Cooper
John & Penny Early
Mike Edge & Pippa England
Stephen Garratt
Rachel Haugh
Richard & Elaine Johnson
Carolyn & Andrew Mellor
Anthony Morrow & Family
Carole Nash OBE
Anthony & Margaret Preston
Nicola Shindler

OUR FIRELIGHTS
John Batley
Mr J Bishop & Mr J Taylor
Sir Robert and Dr Meriel Boyd
Angela Brookes
Paul & Ann Cannings
Mrs V Fletcher
Peter & Judy Folkman
Irene Gray
Roy & Maria Greenwood
Stephen & Arlene Moss
Robin & Mary Taylor
Helen & Phil Wiles

OUR CAMPFIRE MEMBERS: £300
Daniel Bohuslav
John & Kim Fox
Barry Harkison
Geoff Holman
Stella Lowe
Harriet Monkhouse
Mike Smith
Sebastian Taylor
Barry Williams

Thank you to all of our donors who wish to remain anonymous

SHED: EXPLODED VIEW

Phoebe Eclair-Powell

Thanks

My thanks to Alice Birch and all the writers on my writers' group who pushed me to keep going with this idea in 2016. Thank you thank you.

My biggest thanks to Cornelia Parker, whose work, *Cold Dark Matter: An Exploded View* was the inspiration behind all of this and source of continued wonder. Your art is so special to me. Thank you.

To Louise Stephens and Lucy Morrison who taught me about form and content. To Deirdre O'Halloran who made sure this play had an extra life and got me there. Always, always insanely indebted, grateful and lucky to have you in my life. To the whole team at the Bush, for giving me space and time with Sara Joyce, who is a dramaturgical wonder. To Nacho and Luis and your team in Madrid, for letting me see that this play had legs I never knew it had. To the National Theatre Studio, Stewart Pringle and the team who let us all play in 2023 and gave us great notes, a huge thank you. To every single actor who has workshopped this play, you are all extremely generous and I owe all of you a huge, huge debt. Thank you all.

Thanks as ever to my agent Ikenna Obiekwe and his assistant Jess for keeping me on track.

Thank you, Nick Hern and the team, for all your continued support.

Thank you to the Bruntwood, and the generosity of the Bruntwood Award, to Manchester Royal Exchange and all who sail in that glorious spaceship. To Suz. Oh Suz. You are so very, very brilliant and thank you for your fight. To Bryony Shanahan and all the judges of the 2019 award for believing in *Shed*.

To the actors: Jason Hughes, Lizzy Watts, Norah Lopez Holden, Michael Workéyè, Wil Johnson, and Hayley Carmichael.

How insanely lucky I am to work with you epic humans. Thank you for believing and being up for the challenge.

To design heroes: Carmel Smickersgill, Max Pappenheim, Bethany Gupwell, Naomi Dawson, and Sung Im Her. Thanks for making a theatre explode.

To stage management: Amelia Blackburn, Sophie Wright and Amy Bending (and Tash!), and Company Manager Scott.

To Amara Heyland-Morrin, what a star you are.

To Atri, thank you for standing by me, for holding my hand, for being the person I could trust most with this bad boy. I am forever grateful for our partnership, for your mind, soul, talent and kindness.

To my partner, Tris, and my son, Arlo. When I wrote this play I had no idea you would be my solar system. How strange and surreal time is.

P.E-P.

Characters

LIL, *forty-five to seventy-five*
TONY, *fifty to eighty*
NAOMI, *twenty-six to fifty-seven*
FRANK, *thirty to sixty*
ABI, *nought to twenty-six*
MARK, *nineteen to twenty-eight*

Despite family connections the casting does not need to reflect this.

Note on Play

This play is based on Cornelia Parker's *Cold Dark Matter: An Exploded View.*

It is not meant to be naturalistic, even when it is at its most normal.

That does not mean that there isn't emotion and heart.

This play is an explosion in action.

This is one order in which the scenes can work.

The scenes each have titles, so that – if the director and actors wanted to – they could reorder the scenes to fit their production. They can even exclude certain scenes that no longer work for them. However, care should be maintained for the overall arc. You will find a section at the back of the playtext with additional scenes that were not chosen for this production.

Rhythm is important for the overlapping/shared scenes.

The play probably needs some musical handling – like it was a score perhaps.

Note on Text

Talking about musical handling, in rehearsals we decided that lines in bold were to be spoken together, those with an ellipsis (…) before the line were canon (as in said just after the line that features on the same line). The rhythm is paramount, but that's not to say that actors can't start to play with the musicality of the lines to stop it becoming robotic. Lines in italics are private thoughts – but said out loud, if that's what you feel is best.

'Cacophony' needs to be handled the most like a choir/piece of music. Find what works best for you. It needs to build, huge, overwhelming, a mishmash of voices.

This text went to press before the end of rehearsals and so may differ slightly from the play as performed.

HAPPY NEW YEAR – 1993 / 1994

NAOMI.
 Ten
 Nine
 Eight
 Seven
 Six
 Five
 Four

TONY. Will you marry me?

LIL. Yes you bastard.

  She was right – you're nice

FRANK. I knew she'd said something

NAOMI. Of course she did – do you want another? I've hidden some – behind the sofa. I love New Year –

FRANK. Really?

NAOMI. No, I just, I like the fireworks, I really love a firework – the explosion in the sky, the ones that rain –

FRANK. I want this year gone to be honest – bring on 1994

NAOMI. It's been alright actually, I got a / job

FRANK. Will you kiss me at New Year – when the clock strikes will you?

NAOMI.
 Three
 Two
 One

ALL. HAPPY NEW YEAR!

  FRANK *and* NAOMI *kiss. Fireworks.*

  Blackout. In the darkness. A voice:

FORK

NAOMI. There was a fork in her face
   An actual fork
   He dug a fork into her face
   A fork stood on end in her cheek
   A fork
   He stabbed the meat of her face with a fork and for a moment it stood there, stood out
   It reverberated
   A fork

HONEYMOON – 1995

Lights up. 1995.

FRANK. Suncream?

NAOMI. We bought some in – the um

                LIL. Did you see them?

FRANK. So hot in here

NAOMI. Air-con
Just over by the

                TONY. Who the couple next door?

                LIL. Of course the couple next door
Big bloke with the tiny wife

                TONY. Jesus he was monolithic

Just hit the
Over there

                and she looked a bit
Sort of… wet

                LIL. Damp I would say damp

You take so long to
Root yourself

FRANK. Yes

NAOMI. Sorry – I got at you then

                TONY. Damp is the perfect word for her

FRANK. A little perhaps

                Like you could snap her in two
Like you could break her in seconds

                              LIL. She looked positively
                                 drippy
                                 Fancy a mini-fridge beer?

NAOMI. That was mean of me
   Sorry

   I'm just so
   anxious
   For this to be –

FRANK. Perfect

NAOMI. Right

FRANK. I know you are, for
   everything to be –

                              TONY. Look at the prices!
                                 No we'll go to the bar
                                 Go look for some bars

Perfect – Why is that?

                              LIL. We are supposed to
                                 be celebrating – one
                                 mini-fridge beer

                              TONY. Celebrating – what
                                 for?

NAOMI. I don't know

                              LIL. Get out of it

                              TONY. For getting married? –
                                 sorry been there done that –

                              LIL. Charming

   It was a lovely day though

FRANK. Pretty good

NAOMI. Really nice
   It was lovely
   It was a lovely, lovely
   wedding

FRANK. **It didn't rain**	LIL. **It didn't rain**
NAOMI. It's meant to be good luck actually	
	TONY. Never has at my weddings
FRANK. You prayed it wouldn't	
NAOMI. And it didn't Sorry we just We did it again didn't / we	
FRANK. Don't do this	
NAOMI. We could get some more champagne	
FRANK. You drank it all? You little drunkard…	
NAOMI. We could get some more	
	Just a drink – need a good drink
	LIL. To the bar then! To the bar! Jesus
FRANK. Maybe not	
NAOMI. **Do you know what?**	TONY. **Do you know what?**
FRANK. **What?**	LIL. **What?**
NAOMI. I don't feel… I don't feel drunk I don't feel it	TONY. …I don't feel married
	I did the first time – but now, I don't know
	LIL. Nothing at all?
No, nothing at all	

...

LIL. Perfect place for a honeymoon –

NAOMI. I was just saying that – because the warm and the sky

LIL. It's just perfect isn't it?

NAOMI. Really, really perfect

LIL. And you know it's just quiet and calm

NAOMI. Stress-free like they said

LIL. Really actually stress-free

NAOMI. And the beach

LIL. Just perfect

NAOMI. Not too busy

TONY. Lots of couples but you know – no kids

LIL. No – not many kids

NAOMI. So a real young lovers' holiday

TONY. Or old lovers
   Like us

NAOMI. Sorry – no – you're not exactly well –

LIL. Third marriage for him, second for me

NAOMI. Well that's not unusual

LIL. Not at all
   And you're on your first

NAOMI. We are

LIL. Lovely

NAOMI. It was. It was a lovely day

FRANK. Well the weather was a bit
   And your uncle –

NAOMI. Yeah but it was, we both said it was a lovely day, just how lovely it was

LIL. Yes

FRANK. And this hotel is a bit

TONY. I know exactly what you mean

FRANK. Same food every night

NAOMI. It IS good though, it's good food

FRANK. Is it?

NAOMI. I think it's really um…

LIL. The menu is classic
Simple but good quality

FRANK. Hair in my –

NAOMI. It was a mistake – one mistake
It can't always be perfect

LIL. First marriage – how very, very lovely
How very, very, very, very lovely, oh how lovely, isn't it lovely, just look, look at her so lovely and young and lovely she's tiny, she's so tiny – brittle bones look at her sparrow-winged and little dress and big man and down the aisle and here she comes and oh what fun and that smile, a pretty bride, not stunning, no not stunning – but a pretty bride, so little and pretty and big man and lift her up and twirl her round and down and down deep, deep down and on the ground and let's all clap and look and laugh and oh really this song and what fun – and again! Again! And round and down and don't stop, no don't stop – no please stop crying you silly little thing, it's tears of joy, oh such tears of joy and happiness and what a day oh yes a lovely day a perfect day – this day is wonderful she is wonderful what a wonderful couple nothing can ruin this day, no not this day, no nothing can ruin this day, oh oh oh oh how lovely, how very, very, very, very, very, very, very, very, very, very, very, very, very –

TONY. Luv?

LIL. Hmmm

TONY. You're doing it again – zoning out on us
  Too many of these

LIL. Sorry – too relaxed

TONY. To the happy couple
  Cheers

...

NAOMI. The lunch was good. I'm full
  So full
  Just need to lie down and get it all
  Can you just –

                        LIL. I thought he was going to kill her with his eyes

FRANK. What?

                        You saw it didn't you – not one word to each other the whole time

                        TONY. You were staring – you shouldn't stare like that

NAOMI. **Oi**
  Please
                        LIL. **Oi**

                        TONY. He's intense I'll give you that

My tummy, can you just –

FRANK. I'm going for a swim

NAOMI. You can't – you
  have to wait –
  you have to let it digest
  you get cramp –

FRANK. That's not true you
  know, that's not actually
  true
  And I'm a man not a child

                        LIL. Fucking sledgehammer more like
  I mean you've heard them

NAOMI. No I didn't –

                TONY. We've both heard them –

Can you just rub my

I wasn't getting at you –
sorry I thought it was true

                LIL. Something about it
                …it isn't

FRANK. Well it isn't

NAOMI. Right

                …Right

                TONY. I'm a bit jealous if I'm honest

FRANK. Shouldn't have had seconds.

        …

NAOMI. Our last day here

FRANK. Just enjoy it then
We could go for a walk or

NAOMI. We've done that
I'll just pack, yeah think I'll just
Pack now

FRANK. We could do it later

NAOMI. I'll just get it done now
I might go for the chicken tonight, because you had it last night and it looked good –

FRANK. Shall we stop this? Now. Shall we just admit that this

NAOMI. Don't
I'm going to go for a walk actually
Yes a walk
I'm going to go for a walk.
And you should just pack. Yes
Just pack.

...

NAOMI. I'll miss this warm, it really is just so very warm

LIL. First marriages are hard

NAOMI. Maybe all marriages are hard
Sorry I didn't

I want to cry so very badly but there's a couple getting their wedding pictures taken by the sunset and it might ruin the

LIL. A little
Feel the sand instead
Go on really feel it in between your toes
Sand turns to glass
Feel the sharp prick of that sand between your feet and run
Take it from me –
Run.

An aeroplane takes off.

Blackout.

MARK AND ABI – ARE YOU A FRESHER?

2015.

ABI. Hello

MARK. – who are you –
Are you a fresher?

ABI. Is this the bathroom?

    Shit
Sorry

MARK. Here – in the bin

ABI. Thanks
Shit

    Sorry

    This is your bedroom isn't it?

    I'm really drunk

MARK. I can tell

ABI. Can I sit down?

MARK. Um
Yeah
It's sort of out-of-bounds this room

ABI. I know
I saw the sign and thought it might be a spare toilet
Because the other one's blocked up with sick
Because I was maybe a bit sick in it –
I've never been this pissed before

    …
Sorry – just
I'm a virgin
I'm not religious Christian or anything
I'm just a bit like stupid because now I'm at uni and who the fuck goes to uni a virgin

Sorry I might be sick again
nope it's just bile
I didn't have any dinner

Well I did

But it's all come up

MARK. Here
Use this

ABI. That's a T-shirt

MARK. Give a fuck

ABI. Okay
Thanks

Do you wanna have sex with me?

MARK. What –

ABI. I kinda just want to get it over and done with

MARK. Okay

ABI. Yeah?

MARK. Yeah

ABI. I'm Abi by the way

MARK. Oh yeah – Mark
Let me just

Here

ABI. Oh chewing gum
Thanks

SHED 1

2024.

NAOMI *is making a shed. It's a 'build your own shed' pack.*

FRANK. Naomi?
 What are you doing –
 It's late

 Is this all B&Q?
 Did you drive to B&Q this morning?
 Are you really doing this now?
 Do we even need a shed?

PREGNANT / I GAVE HER AWAY

1996.

FRANK. **You're sure?**	TONY. **You're sure**
NAOMI. **Yes**	LIL. **Yes**
	I'm far too old Did you want one – really?
FRANK. Really?! Well… okay… that's great! That's – we should –	
	TONY. No I just… well I didn't with the other two
Do we tell people or	
	LIL. They're not numbers, they have names!
	TONY. Tweedledum and Tweedledee…
	LIL. Oi –
NAOMI. Maybe not for a bit	
	TONY. and well I thought maybe – women your age sometimes…
Just in case	
	LIL. very rarely. Anyway I had one before
FRANK. This is a bit mad	
	TONY. Oh You didn't tell me
NAOMI. I know!	LIL.…No I know Sorry
	TONY. None of my business –
FRANK. Can I say hello?	

NAOMI It's not even – it's
just cells now so

                              LIL. I gave her away
                                  When she was born
                                So I don't

But we should think of
names

                              …I don't even know her
                              name

FRANK. Right, fuck   TONY.…Right
Right then   **Right then**
That's… that's
Right then
I love you

NAOMI. I love you too

FRANK. What about, what
about Abigail?

NAOMI. It might not be a girl

FRANK. I think it's a girl
I think I want a girl

NOT ALL MEN / PINT – HALF-PINT

2016.

FRANK. **I'm just saying it's not all men**	MARK. **I'm just saying it's not all men**
	ABI. No I know it's no/t –
Three women raped that footballer the other day	MARK. **Three women raped that guy the other day**
NAOMI. No I know that	
	ABI. I saw that in the um –
	MARK. *Daily Mail* –
FRANK. In the *Mail* yes	
NAOMI. *Daily Mail*, yes but that is very, very highly unusual and	
	Fucking mental I mean fucking hell
FRANK. psycho fucking bitches	
NAOMI. Yes well they were clearly a bit	
	ABI. – American right?
FRANK. High as fucking kites and pure fucking evil.	
	MARK. I mean that poor guy
	ABI. He didn't testify did he –
	MARK. Fuck no – I mean embarrassing that – truly kacked yourself pants down embarrassing that. So do you want another drink then or

ABI. Yeah go on

MARK. Pint

ABI. Half

MARK. Don't believe in halves

ABI. You always say that

MARK. Automatic – want one or not

ABI. Fine

MARK. Pint or half-pint

ABI. Thought you didn't

Pint

MARK. What

ABI. I just

MARK. What

ABI. I thought the other day that maybe

MARK. What?

ABI. Shut up
Nothing

MARK. No way – are you

ABI. I'm not
I don't think so
I'm just

MARK. You've been eating a lot

ABI. Fuck's sake

MARK. And you've been really fucking moody

Okay
Right then

ABI. Shit
Shit

MARK. Okay
I'll just get a half then

ABI. Just a half

MARK *goes, he returns with drinks*

There's cot death and colic
and croup and infections,
viruses, meningitis, car
accident, car crash,
choking, concussion,
internal bleeding,
pneumonia, allergic
reaction, childhood
cancers, rare genetic
disorders, drowning,
kidnap, paedophiles, online
grooming, poison,
bullying, anorexia, bulimia,
self-harm, depression,
suicide, speeding, terrorist
attacks, overdose,
and whooping cough and
no face and no teeth and no
eyes and no mouth and no
bones and no ribs and just
a mess – it comes out a
mess, I can't birth a mess.
I'm sorry but no

No
Actually I've decided no
Just no

MARK. Okay – it's your

ABI. No
So just no

MARK. Okay
We'll… Just… I mean if you're sure

ABI. I mean yes

MARK. Because we could make really –

ABI. No

MARK. Okay then –

ABI. We haven't even finished uni

MARK. No

ABI. and my course is shit –

MARK. I know

ABI. And your house is Fucking –

MARK. / Yes alright

ABI. Shit
And I mean look at us – we're a fucking joke

MARK. That's a bit –

ABI. I mean just no

MARK. I said okay, I don't know what you want me to –

ABI. That easily – Just like that

MARK. No – not just like that – what are you saying – this doesn't have to be a big deal. I don't even know what you're saying

ABI. Really – really? I'm saying – how can you just be like okay – you're only okay – because it's what you want isn't it –
Is it what you want?
Isn't it?

MARK. Yes, it's what I want

BABY ABI

1997.

NAOMI (*to baby Abi*). No baby Abi silly baby Abi, silly silly
   goose thing, tiny mouseling child my little moo –
   it goes one banana two banana
   three banana four…
   four bananas make a bunch
   and so do many more
   doo doo doo doo doo dooo

   please stop crying now
   please
   I would rip you in two if I could if you could just please
   I want to die I want to die I want to fucking die
   One banana two banana three banana four
   Dooo dooo dooo doo doo dooo doo

LOST MY JOB / FIRED

2007.

FRANK. I lost my job

                                          TONY. Fired

NAOMI. Your job –

FRANK. I lost my fucking
   job, they said…   …They said I was

They said   forgetting things –
I would have to reapply
you know
I thought I was just
reapplying for
my job, that's all
They did it as a group

NAOMI. **What?**   LIL. **What?**

FRANK. They did a group
   firing
Not even an individual
meeting
There were five of us
It was like a game show
A shit game show
And I
I don't get anything   TONY.…I don't get it – I
No redundancy no nothing
I get

NAOMI. Surely
   Pension
   Bit of – something maybe

FRANK. I get

   Fuck   **Fuck**

   I can't even think

                                          Forgetting things

NAOMI. **We'll sort it**

LIL. **We'll sort it.**

FRANK. You don't know how this feels you don't do anything –

NAOMI. I can imagine it's very hard to –

FRANK. No you don't have any – you don't know this
I liked my job

TONY. **I liked my job**

NAOMI. **You were good at your job, you'll find –**

LIL. **You were good at your job, you'll find** another

FRANK. Really find another – were you going to say find another

TONY. You're right – I'll find another

NAOMI. I didn't mean it like that

LIL. Fucking ballache though

FRANK. Fuck… her lessons We can't have the lessons She doesn't need them

NAOMI. You need to just You've had something to drink so maybe you should –

FRANK. Really – right now –

TONY. …right now it's a fucking ballache

NAOMI. I'm not saying there's anything wrong with / that

FRANK. I wanted to have more than this and now I won't get it

Can you just…
I just wanted her to have
things, to have everything.

NAOMI.…**I'm here**	LIL. Well, **I'm here**
FRANK. **Can you just**	TONY. **Can you just**
Not make that fucking face at me	
	…Hold me –
	LIL. Of course, come here
Fucking hell The shame You want me to die of it I really can't I just Cancel her fucking lessons.	TONY.… I just –
	LIL. I'm here.
	TONY. I know
Sorry…	
NAOMI. I know	

MUM. MUM. MUM

Kitchen, 1999.

ABI. Mum, Mum, Mum, Mum, Mum, Mum, Mum, Mum, Mum, Mum, Mum, Mum

Kitchen, 2003.

Mum, Mum, Mum, Mum, Mum, Mum, Mum, Mum, Mum, Mum, Mum, Mum

Kitchen, 2006.

Mum, Mum, Mum, Mum, Mum, Mum, Mum, Mum, Mum, Mum, Mum, Mum

Kitchen, 2010.

Mum, Mum, Mum, Mum, Mum, Mum, Mum, Mum, Mum, Mum, Mum, Mum

Kitchen, 2012.

Mum, Mum, Mum, Mum, Mum, Mum, Mum, Mum, Mum, Mum, Mum, Mum
Why are you so boring?

SHATTERED GLASS

2006.

NAOMI *drops a glass. It shatters.*

NAOMI. Sorry I um – broke a glass

FRANK. So you stood on it?

NAOMI. I wanted to… yes.

   FRANK *gets a dustpan and brush, he cleans up the glass.*

WHO ARE YOU TEXTING?

2020.

MARK. **Who you texting?**	NAOMI. **Who are you texting?**
ABI. Not, just scrolling	
	FRANK. I'm not – no one
MARK. You were typing	
	NAOMI. You're literally typing
ABI. Because I was commenting on a thing	
MARK. Texting someone	
	you were texting someone –
ABI. No just commenting	
MARK. On what	
	Texting her?
ABI. For like a prize thing	
MARK. **For what**	**For what –**
ABI. Like a prize	
MARK. To win what	
ABI. Christ like a spa weekend thing for me and Janey	
MARK. You don't like fat Janey	
ABI. I do like fat – **fuck** Mark don't	FRANK. **Fuck**
MARK. Fat Janeeeeeey Go on then – delete it	NAOMI. ...delete it, delete her number

ABI. **What**

MARK. Because it's bollocks

ABI. **It's not**

MARK. You're **fucking obsessed with your phone** –

    Give it

ABI. Mark!

MARK. **Jesus** what is this photo

    You look mental
    why you trying to be
    a fucking Kardashian
    Pouting
    Christ
    State

ABI. Give it back Mark

MARK. Tits all smushed up like a prozzie
I'm joking – **sex worker**.

    But **delete it**
    No honestly I'm doing you a favour
    Delete it

    ABI *deletes it*.

    Good girl.
    FAT JANNEEEEEEY
    God she's annoying

FRANK. **What**

    …this is bollocks

NAOMI. **It's not**

    fucking obsessed with your phone

    Give it to me –

FRANK.…Naomi –

    Jesus

    It's just a photo don't go mental

    Christ

    give it back Naomi

NAOMI. fucking **sex worker** –
delete it

FRANK.…I'll delete it

YOU PROMISED ME

1999.

LIL. So you lied to me

TONY. No, it's just

LIL. Because my card was declined Tony
   And our shared account
   There's hardly anything in it
   And you said that there was nothing wrong
   When we met
   You promised me
   That there was none of that
   That shit
   That there always is
   And I like a fucking idiot
   Believed you
   But you were lying

TONY. I… I made a mistake
   It's not a big deal
   I always manage it
   And I do well
   And I don't lose big and I don't win big
   And it's usually fine
   And this was just a blip
   One mistake
   A stupid bet
   Just one
   A one-off
   I'll get it back
   I'll win it back
   And

LIL. It was thousands of pounds

TONY. It's honestly not that much
   We can get past this right – Lil

LIL. I… I

TONY. Come on
It was just one mistake
It won't happen again
It was just once
I swear
Oh come on –
Don't make that face
The shame
Do you want me to die of it
I don't know what you want me to do
I said I'm sorry
I'm not having this conversation

I'm not having it right now
I've had it up to here and I

I think we should just
Lil…

Please I'm sorry

LIL. I know…

TONY. Come here
It won't happen again
I promise
I promise
How else do you think we have what we have.

HIT ME BABY ONE MORE TIME

2005.

NAOMI. No just give me another chance and I'll do it right
this time
Promise
Oh go on
Please
Abi
Show me
Show me one more time

ABI. Fine

She does a dance routine.

Hit me baby one more time
And then you go – urgh

NAOMI. Okay urgh – like that

ABI. Yeah but more like – like do it properly

NAOMI. I am!
Okay okay
Hit me baby one more time.
URGH
I did it!
Don't laugh at me
Are you laughing at me

Come on one more time

BOTH. HIT ME BABY ONE MORE TIME – URGH

NAOMI. Yes
I did it
High-five
Oh come on
High-five

ABI. One more –

BOTH. HIT ME BABY ONE MORE TIME – URGH

SHED – 2

2024.

FRANK. Are you really doing this now?
Do we even need a shed?

Look, I know today was… hard. But this isn't the right –
We should be inside
Maybe
Just together
and
You don't put that there, I don't think – here let me just –
We don't have very good tools do we
Naomi – are you listening –
Naomi?

WHEN YOU FIRST HAVE SEX / IT WILL KILL YOU

2012.

NAOMI. and when you first, um, when you first have sex there's going to be this um – maybe like a pain, because you see you're breaking this um thing, sorry not breaking, um, what's a better word – sort of popping through a bit of skin, a sort of bit of – this really tiny not-important thing, called a hymen – breaks – sorry not breaks, sort of um goes and it might feel like ooh ah – but for a bit and then it's all – you know then it's fine, and you know – there might be some blood –

ABI. I know all this
Jesus

NAOMI. Right
So I'll just

ABI. If you leave those there
I will kill you

                                      LIL. It will kill you

NAOMI. There

ABI. I will kill you
I hate you I hate you I hate
you.

                                      Oh
                                      How do we do this.

                                    TONY. I
                                        I know
                                        But
                                        It's okay
                                        Don't panic
                                        Because panic is not
                                        Is not
                                        We're not to panic

They said ten years some
people
I don't want you to panic
Or cry
Or panic
Because we can't
We can't
We just can't

LIL. I don't want to watch
you disappear.

THEY HURT YOU

2019.

ABI. Oh my god Mark – your face
  Your face is bleeding

  How did this happen –
  Are you okay
  Shit sit down
  Should I call someone or
  Here – water
  You're shaking
  What happened
  Your jacket – it's all ripped?

MARK. I was mugged
  Coming out the station

ABI. Oh Mark – shit
  Your phone –

MARK. Gone
  I tried to grab it back so he
  He and his mate
  They
  And it was really quick
  And suddenly I'm on the floor
  And this fucking businessman is helping me up
  But he doesn't want to get the blood on his suit
  So he just sort of gestures at me to get up
  And then runs for his train

ABI. and no one else helped you or –
  or called someone?

MARK. of course not
  cos I'm fine
  it just looks worse than it is
  the cunts
  the fucking

ABI. You can cry Mark
   You're allowed to

MARK. I'm fine.

   It was nothing
   Nothing happened
   I'm fine.

NEW YEAR – HE JUMPED

1999 / 2000.

NAOMI. He jumped – right in front of me, not in front, he was a bit further up the platform, but he, and this woman screamed and some people coming down the stairs panicked and ran back up and it was so quick but the sound of it braking is really like – like it really hurts your ears. I was um, yeah it was – I can't believe that happened when I was there, because you never think you'll actually be there, to witness it. I just think – fuck you must really hate your life, because that is not a guarantee you know – like you could just end up… mangled.
I think it's the hysteria – they say that – of a new start – a millennium – all this millennium bug nonsense – it's just too much, they say that don't they – that the New Year is when people kill themselves, when people end it – because it's a tipping point, like do I do this? – do I carry on like this, because the dates just keep on coming, the days keep hurtling at you – and

FRANK. I can't watch this when you're talking

NAOMI. Sorry

FRANK. Love Jools Holland

                                    LIL. HAPPY NEW YEAR –

                                    TONY. And anniversary

                                    LIL. Not really our anniversary
                                              That's the wedding isn't it

                                      He suddenly drifts.

                                      Tony?

                                    TONY. Hmm

                                    LIL. You okay?

                                    TONY. Just felt cold

                                    LIL. Get you a jumper

                                    TONY. No, no, I'm fine, I'll
                                              be fine

EAT SOMETHING

2014.

NAOMI. How was school?

ABI. Fine

NAOMI. Say more than that

ABI. Mostly fine

   Can I go to my room?

NAOMI. No, dinner's nearly ready

ABI. **I don't want to eat**	TONY. **I don't want to eat**

NAOMI. Stop this
  You're having food
  I've made food
	LIL. **You're having food**
	  I've made food
	  Please try

FRANK. Listen to your mum.
  You can **have a bit**
 	
  Don't pressurise her – you know we're not supposed to
	Have a bit

ABI. It smells weird, it's fucking rank	
	TONY. It smells like shit

NAOMI. **Right**,
  do you know what actually go to your room
	LIL. **Right**
	  …for fuck's sake

ABI *goes.*	
Sorry, I just **can't go through this again.**	**can't go through this again –**
I just want her to be happy	

FRANK. She'll be okay…

NAOMI. I'll go up and check on her

FRANK. **No** – you know we're not supposed to – they told us not to do that

LIL. **No…**

Don't do that – come on, you know how to eat, you do, you do remember this, you can do this. Please just fucking EAT JUST FUCKING EAT IT YOU FUCKING –

LIL *throws the food at the wall.*

What even is it?

NAOMI. Moussaka

sorry I…

FRANK. It does smell a bit weird.

…

I'll go up and check on her.

I'll do it then.

I'll do it

ARE YOU SERIOUSLY JUST GOING TO SHUT THE FUCK UP

2002.

FRANK. Are you? No but are you seriously really seriously just going to shut the fuck up, just shut the fuck up, for once in your fucking life, going to just stop, stop the argument stop it dead, because it's over it's actually over and fuck off I can see your lips moving, your brain thinking – you are going to open your fucking mouth and say something aren't you – you're actually going to fucking say something. Just don't, just don't, just fucking don't. Jesus. No wonder I hate you so fucking much you absolute piece of fucking shit in my life. My life is so shit. My life is so fucking shit.

WE WATCHED THEM BUCKLE

2015.

NAOMI. We stood in a park and we watched them buckle, great big slabs of concrete just buckle asunder till the dust cloud was so big it reached up to meet it and you couldn't even see if it was, if it was even falling any more.
And I couldn't stop thinking about this woman who was left in a lift when the builders shut it off – in Japan. She suffocated eventually or starved. It took ages apparently. It took a really long time

Don't you remember?
The building – you were only little

ABI. No

NAOMI. But we watched it, a whole building collapse,
we saw the – the insides – the
curtains and the wallpaper

                                    LIL. You collapsed, you went
                                    so white you

ABI. I told you – no, I

NAOMI. **Hold my hand**   TONY. **Hold my hand**

ABI. Why you being weird

NAOMI. **Please**   **Please**
                                        Hold my hand

                                        I love your hands. Your
                                        hands make me feel like
                                        I am anchored to the
                                        ground, like a kid holding
                                        a balloon. If I hold your
                                        hand, I am okay. Just hold
                                        my hand. Hold it, hold it
                                        tight and close to me, don't
                                        let it go, no whatever you
                                        do please don't let it go.
                                        Don't let me go.

                    LIL. Tony you're hurting
                        me – please

                    Tony, my hand – Tony?

                    TONY. Sorry I… I'm so sorry

I love you

ABI. Shut up, I love you too

SHED – 3

2024.

NAOMI *is building a shed, it is about a quarter of the way there.*

FRANK. Naomi – are you listening –
   Naomi?

   You know my dad had a shed
   Full of porn
   No, I mean some porn, and some spades and some fertiliser
   And then all the alcohol
   But not for a while
   Not until Mum died
   My mum died when I was seven
   I suddenly really um – it's like I only just realised that – that seven is quite young
   You always used to say that made me more lovable
   Lost boy
   Peter Pan
   I think it made me quite cruel actually

   I once saw him dancing on his own in the kitchen, Dad, think he was pretending he was dancing with her
   Mum liked a slow dance
   Big fan of Billy Fury

   I watched him for ages
   And he looked really… calm
   so eventually I walked over
   And he had his eyes closed
   And I danced with him

   We never spoke about it
   I just remembered that

   Naomi?
   It didn't rain…

   I'll go make us a drink…

FRANK AND ABI

2007.

ABI. I don't want to ride it any more

FRANK. What?

ABI. The bike I don't want to

FRANK. What happened

ABI. Nothing

FRANK. Your knee

ABI. I just scraped it

FRANK. That was expensive Abi
   You can't just give up because you got hurt
   You have to try again
   Things take time
   Work
   Energy
   effort
   You can't just give in like that Abi
   Abi

ABI. They said they could see my pants, so they threw things at me. And then I fell.

FRANK. Oh, right then.

SHATTERED GLASS – 2

2006 and 2013.

NAOMI *drops a glass. It shatters.* TONY *drops a glass. It shatters.*

NAOMI. **Sorry I um – broke a glass**	TONY. **Sorry I um – broke a glass**
	LIL. Tony?
FRANK. So you stood on it	
NAOMI. I wanted to… yes.	
	TONY. I can't feel my hands

DO YOU THINK THEY LOVE EACH OTHER? / CHUBBY MONKEY

2018.

ABI. what would your mates say if they knew you combed my hair like this?

MARK. I just like it

ABI. Your little ritual

MARK. I know

ABI. You've always liked it

MARK. It's not weird
It's just so smooth

ABI. My mum made me grow my hair

MARK. I don't like short hair on girls

ABI. I know you don't babe
Every night sat here like this and you stroking my hair
Getting your fingers in there

Making it greasy

MARK. I don't

ABI. You do

MARK. Do I

ABI. Yeah – Ow!

MARK. Sorry, there was a knot…

ABI. Do you think they love each other?

MARK. what

ABI. your parents

MARK. no idea

ABI. I think mine don't

MARK. What

ABI. I think they're just sort of meh
Does that just happen

MARK. I dunno

ABI. Like does everyone just get bored or

MARK. Your dad fucks other women and your mum can't be bothered
I think it works quite well

ABI. Yeah maybe you're right.
I liked our first date
Do you remember?

MARK. The cinema

ABI. No that pizza place
You were amazed when I ate the whole thing – stuffed crust
And a milkshake

MARK. you're my chubby monkey
Come here monkey
Rub that big belly

ABI. Oi
I swear it was the pizza

MARK. No
No it was definitely the cinema

ABI. You're wrong
It was right after that party
Where I met you
And then the next day

MARK. I've told you, you're wrong.

ABI. What film was it then?

MARK. It was… fuck

ABI. Ha, see you can't remember, and then after the pizza we had sex for the first time

MARK. No, we had sex when we met at the party

ABI. Did we?

MARK. Yeah – You were fucked.

FIFTY – HENRY

2017.

NAOMI. Can you get the mini-quiches out of the fridge

MARK. I will

NAOMI. Thank you / Mark

ABI. Really?

NAOMI. What

ABI. Mini-quiche

NAOMI. I like mini-quiche

ABI. Look at Mum go
Fifty and she finally gives in to the mini-quiche
Fuck it's so hot today

NAOMI. Careful

MARK. sorry
I'm so sorry

NAOMI. It's fine
No it's –

ABI. No it is fine you've had this carpet for years

NAOMI. Go and serve it to people

ABI. It's just cousin Charlotte and weirdo Colin who voted for Brexit

NAOMI. Don't bring that up just go and – fine I'll do it with you –

....

They leave.
MARK *and* FRANK *are alone...*

FRANK. So you guys alright

MARK. Yeah
Yeah

FRANK. Great
How's uni?

MARK. Alright
　Yeah
　Lot of work

FRANK. Yeah, all work no play – feel sorry for your lot, lot of pressure

MARK. Yeah

FRANK. Do you want another beer or – or a wine or
　Think there's some fizzy stuff somewhere
　Or

MARK. Nah I'm alright

FRANK. Right
　Might just have another

　You er –

The women return.

ABI. he brought it up – not me –

MARK. Can I use your toilet?

ABI. You don't have to ask to use the toilet it's not school, but go get the thing – from the car

MARK. But I actually do need a piss

An exchange – MARK *leaves.*

ABI. You don't look fifty

NAOMI. Thank you

　MARK *re-enters.*

ABI. Did you bring it then?

NAOMI. What?

ABI. Nothing

NAOMI. Finally – am I getting a present

FRANK. Oh yeah it's in the –

ABI. Mark got it Dad

NAOMI. Come on then

FRANK. Here we go

ABI. You better like it

NAOMI. I will like it

ABI. No you really better like it

FRANK. It's a
It's a…

NAOMI. Hoover

FRANK. New Henry!

ABI. Gettit

FRANK. Cos you loved the old one – and you got all upset when we got you the
You know
Non-Henry and you said you missed his face

NAOMI. Did I

ABI. Yeah – you like mourned for Henry
So we got you Henry

NAOMI. Right
He's lovely
Really
So yellow

ABI. So I can have the other one you didn't like
Which is good cos ours is broken

NAOMI. Yeah
Yeah it's
No that's

ABI. Look you can test it out on his quiche

HOOVER – STARING

2016.

TONY *is staring at the hoover.*

LIL. It's just the hoover

TONY. Staring at me – it's
What's it saying?

LIL. It's okay – come back to bed. Tony – please come back to bed
Tony –
Tony darling

TONY. *Are you? No but are you seriously really seriously just going to shut the fuck up, just shut the fuck up, for once in your fucking life, going to just stop stop the argument stop it dead, because it's over it's actually over and fuck off I can see your lips moving, your brain thinking – you are going to open your fucking mouth and say something aren't you – you're actually going to fucking say something. Just don't, just don't, just fucking don't. Jesus. No wonder I hate you so fucking much you absolute piece of fucking shit in my life. My life is so shit. My life is so fucking shit.*

I'm sorry… I don't know where I am

GRADUATION / ONCE

2019.

BIG LAUGH.

NAOMI. I wish you could've seen it
She looked hilarious and this one kid – well he had sick all down his gown –
Oh that gown and cape thing and god it went on but I just thought – well done, well done and, and I know she didn't do as well as we hoped, but she's got this piece of paper now and well she's sort of passed over – to another stage hasn't she and I thought – what the fuck do I do now...
Like who am I now.

How was the work trip?

FRANK. Fine –

NAOMI. ...Did you see her again?

FRANK. No

NAOMI. Don't lie

FRANK. Once.

NAOMI. I don't know what you expect me to feel.
It's like a wound you keep picking and –

FRANK. I... I was saying goodbye. Like you wanted – / we didn't

NAOMI. like 'I wanted'

FRANK. we talked about this – we agreed / that –

NAOMI. I don't give a shit about what we agreed – I just feel fucking annoyed okay and betrayed

FRANK. You said to be honest, I'm being honest, I've ended it, I've ended it for you

NAOMI. And I'm supposed to be grateful –

FRANK. You never cared before

NAOMI. Well this time, this time for some reason I care,
    I fucking care okay and I –

FRANK. I've said I'm sorry I'm sorry – I am, it won't happen again – I do love you Naomi. I love you and I love Abi.

NAOMI. No don't try and hug me
    Try and make this all okay with
    Just fuck off –

FRANK. Did you just push me?!
    If I pushed you
    If I so much as touched you
    Fucking dare you.

NAOMI. I'm sorry…
    I…
    I'm tired
    I'm so tired

We have a nice life. We have a nice life I suppose. I…

FRANK. did you take any pictures –

NAOMI. oh… yeah, here…

FRANK. …
    I'm so proud of her…

NAOMI. I know.

NO IT'S FINE

2023.

ABI. No it's fine
   It wasn't like I was
   It was only a few weeks
   We hadn't even told Mum and Dad yet
   So
   It doesn't even really count

MARK. Is it my fault?

ABI. No
   Not at all

MARK. I pushed you

ABI. But that's not
   It wouldn't have
   Don't cry
   Please don't cry there, there
   Come on
   Let's just go back to bed
   I've cleaned it up
   Let's just go back to sleep.

MARK. I love you so much
   I'm so sorry
   I'm so sorry

ABI. I'm here…
   I'm here…

HIT ME BABY ONE MORE TIME

2005.

They do the dance routine

ABI/NAOMI. HIT ME BABY ONE MORE TIME – URGH

THEY SAID CANCER

2019.

ABI. **I lost my job**
I lost my
fucking job
They said
They said all
this stuff

LIL. **I lost my job**

NAOMI.... They
said cancer

MARK. You hated
that job

ABI. That's not the
point

MARK. I'm just
saying you
hated that job

ABI. **I don't know
what to do**

FRANK. **I don't
know what
to do**

LIL. They said
I was taking too
much time away
to care for you

They said –
they said they
were
restructuring,
I'm just part of
something
way bigger,
**like I'm just
nothing,
not important.**
Like I was
**getting in the
way.**

**like I'm just
nothing
not important**

**getting in the
way**

	NAOMI.… We'll be fine.
MARK. We're fine I work	
ABI. That's not enough though – I want to work, I have to work	
MARK. Then get another job No big deal	…No big deal really,
TONY. what's for lunch?	so many women get this
ABI. No I know it's just	
MARK. Fucking blessing in disguise	
ABI. But the rent – I	
MARK. Shouldn't have got fired then.	
	It'll be fine.
	FRANK. I'll ring her…
	NAOMI. No, not yet, I just want her to be happy
LIL. soup	

MALDIVES

2019.

LIL. You all strapped in
  Comfortable

NAOMI. As I can be

LIL. It's a bit intense the first few times
  You got something to distract you
  Or you can watch something on your phone
  Maybe
  Music is good
  Audiobooks

NAOMI. Sorry I… have we met

LIL. I don't think so – unless I was here last time

NAOMI. You're a nurse

LIL. Yes sweetheart – though not for much longer

NAOMI. Retiring?

LIL Something like that
  You feeling okay?

NAOMI. I… no I'm finding it hard
  sorry I just thought I had met you before years ago
  Maldives
  My honeymoon

LIL. Oh my gosh – that's no you're right
  I… that was years ago

NAOMI. How are you
  You still?

LIL. Oh yeah
  He's… we're… okay – good

NAOMI. We had a little girl
  She's not little sorry she's a grown-up

LIL. I'm sorry to see you here
  Of all places

NAOMI. Yeah. Yes, it's been...
　But I'm lucky
　Early enough

LIL. That's good
　That's really good

NAOMI. That beach was so lovely

LIL. Yeah and the hotel
　Was

NAOMI. Perfect
　Really really perfect.

LIL. You didn't run did you...

NAOMI. No.

STI

2017.

NAOMI. **This is unusual, we haven't had**	LIL. **This is unusual We haven't had sex in a while**	ABI. **We haven't had sex in a while**
		MARK. I thought that's what you wanted
		ABI. It's just you gave me that STI and
		MARK. Every. Fucking. Time.
FRANK. **Could you maybe just –**	**Could you maybe just**	ABI. **Maybe just**
NAOMI. **What?**	TONY. **what?**	MARK. **what?**
FRANK. **Put your hands sort of**	LIL. **Put your hands sort of**	ABI. **put your hands sort of**
NAOMI. **Oh** choke you	TONY. **Oh**	
FRANK. **A little**	LIL. **A little** …are you okay, are you sure Tony?	
NAOMI. Are you trying –		
FRANK. Not to breathe		
NAOMI. You know that funeral I went to the other day? I went in and it was so small.		

And I felt so embarrassed about how small it was that I		
FRANK. **I'm trying to**		MARK. **I'm trying to –**
Just, can you **a bit harder**	LIL. **A bit harder**	
NAOMI. Yes So I **left** I just **left**	…Yes **left** **left**	…No –
Sorry are you	TONY.…are you	ABI.…Are you – oh
FRANK. Yes.		
	LIL.…YES	MARK.…NO
		ABI. it's not a big deal. It happens –
		Mark? Mark…

HAPPY NEW YEAR 2023/24

FRANK. **I'm going to bed**	ABI. **I'm going to bed**	
NAOMI. But you can't – **it's nearly midnight**	MARK. But you can't **it's nearly midnight**	LIL. **nearly midnight**, can't sleep can't stop thinking

    I think
    I think it's thirty years since we met

FRANK. Thirty
    What's that then –

                      ABI. but I'm too tired

NAOMI. Pearl
    Never liked pearls
    Like eyes
    Dead eyes

                      MARK. come on – dance with me

FRANK. Night –

                                            I miss you like an ache.
                                            Happy New Year Tony, wherever you are

                      Ten
                      Nine
                      Eight
                      Seven

ABI/MARK.
Six
Five
Four
Three
Two
One

| NAOMI. **Happy fucking New Year** | **Happy fucking New Year!!!!** | **Happy fucking New Year** |

DRUNK LITTLE FEMINIST BITCH

2019.

MARK. That fucking prick

ABI. what – who?

MARK. that girl who was on our table

ABI. what? Who – but we just had a nice time, you just said it was a really great
Time

MARK. Yeah, it was, until that drunk little feminist bitch told me off for
What what
What was I doing
What was it she said
And you just sat there
Staring at her

ABI. – but you laughed.

MARK. Of course I laughed, I had to fucking laugh – everyone was just staring at me –
you were staring at me

ABI. I was just shocked, confused
I couldn't believe she was

MARK. Like you agreed with her

ABI. I wasn't
I didn't
I didn't even know what she was saying
So I can't even
How can I say something when I can't even really hear what she's saying

MARK. If a man did that – to you, if a guy did that to you, told you off like some patronising schoolteacher like a prick
I would jump in and smash his teeth out in seconds, I would be down his throat I would crawl down his throat in seconds.
I wouldn't even care to listen and yet you sat there
Swear you nodded at one point swear you nodded

ABI. She was just being
She was probably a bit drunk it wasn't a big deal –

MARK. A big deal
We had to leave early

ABI. We didn't have to – you said you were tired

MARK. What? sit next to her after that
After she tells me what I can and can't say

ABI. Sorry.

MARK. Are you though?

ABI. Yes
Sorry
I'm really sorry
Sorry.

MARK. Are you though?
Are you?
But are you seriously –
But are you seriously just going to shut the fuck up just shut the fuck up, for once in your fucking life, going to just stop, stop the argument stop it dead, because it's over it's actually over and fuck off I can see your lips moving, your brain thinking – you are going to open your fucking mouth and say something aren't you – you're actually going to fucking say something. Just don't, just don't, just fucking don't. Jesus. No wonder I hate you so fucking much you absolute piece of fucking shit in my life. My life is so shit. My life is so fucking shit.

IT WAS RAINING

2005.

BIG LAUGH.

LIL. It was raining

TONY. No it wasn't

LIL. It was *cos* I got my umbrella tangled in a businessman's legs and he shouted at me
Full in the face
Spitting
Late for his train
And I was late to meet you and my hair was wet and

TONY. I thought it was sunny

LIL. That's because you met me
And the sky shone

TONY. Eh like angels
Like god having a wink at me from the sky

LIL. Like Apollo was saying 'get in'
But actually it just kept raining and we stayed in that café for hours
I wasn't wearing any pants

TONY. What

LIL. I wasn't

I like to do that on a date

Makes you feel like you've got a secret – and men like you more when they think they can get something out of you – pry something secret out of you

They sense there's more going on

It's true

That's the only reason you wanted me

TONY. I wanted all of you

LIL. We fell out over Thatcher

TONY. Let's not bring that up

LIL. You were still married

TONY. I was
    I feel bad about that

LIL. Yeah right… Tony?

TONY. Hmmm

LIL. Please don't leave me

BOOK CLUB

2017.

NAOMI. We had such a great time, honestly they were all so nice and funny and then this one woman she –	LIL. We had such a great time they're all so nice
FRANK. It's only a book club – you didn't even finish the book	
	you were missed…
	TONY. I find the conversation, too many new faces –
	LIL. I know
NAOMI. Well that's what I was saying – **this one woman – she got the wrong / one**	**this one woman – she got the wrong song**
FRANK. **I'm going to bed**	TONY. **I'm going to bed**
	LIL. Of course…
NAOMI. It was…	
I really	**I really**
I enjoyed myself	**I enjoyed myself**
I had a lovely time	**I had a lovely time**
Hello	
This is my voice	**This is my voice**
This is it	
Here	
My voice	**My voice**

SHED – 4

2024.

FRANK. this is stupid you know that
the neighbours must think you're mental –
come inside
maybe try and eat something

> Why is my laptop out here – you can't keep it out here it might rain
> why's the radio out here?
> It's like a fucking junk shop.
> Is that the hoover?
> That hoover still works Naomi –
> I don't understand why you're building a shed for the hoover –

> Is that all her old stuff, you can't move all her old stuff Naomi
> I don't understand what you're doing –

GARDENING

2022.

ABI. since when did you do gardening?

NAOMI. I wanted to plant something
    To learn to plant something
    To care about something

ABI. Okay

NAOMI. To grow things

ABI. Nothing's going to grow in this heat Mum

NAOMI. Your lot worry about everything
    Anxiety – you all have anxiety
    You take too many pills for things
    We never had that

ABI. You should have had that
    And therapy

NAOMI. Who has time for therapy
    How do you all have time for therapy
    and going to the gym
    That just wasn't a thing I swear

ABI. Mr Motivator
    Do you remember him

NAOMI. Oh yeah

ABI. See *you* had a leotard phase I swear

NAOMI. Pilates – that was big when I had you
    Lots of lying down

ABI. People use machines now

NAOMI. get them. It's not really about exercise, it's about what you eat

ABI. Jesus

NAOMI. I didn't say anything

ABI. You looked

NAOMI. I'm just meaning more – you know we dieted
Your lot are obsessed with taste, everything has to taste really good

ABI. Jesus

NAOMI. No it's true

ABI. You're just a shit cook

NAOMI. Yeah
Dad's good
When he bothers
The hours I have spent in supermarkets
Thinking about food I don't want to have to bother cooking

ABI. Yeah
We just get takeaway

NAOMI. You gunna help or what

ABI. Nah
I'll just sit here

NAOMI. Pass me the spade

ABI. Do you know what you're doing?

NAOMI. YouTube

ABI. Excellent
What are they?

NAOMI. tulips

ABI. sure you should do it like that

NAOMI. yep
fuck off
you're laughing at me

ABI. you're being a bit old lady –
what's this about

NAOMI. I'm trying to be interested in things
In my life

    In my surroundings
    I'm trying to care
    About stuff
    Okay

ABI. Okay
    I get it
    …
    You haven't said anything

NAOMI. What about

ABI. The wedding – setting a date

NAOMI. Not like I don't know him
    Not new news

ABI. It is new news
    This is it
    The man
    The person I share it with
    Do the kid thing with

NAOMI. If you can have them

ABI. If I can have them
    You've always said that

NAOMI. I just don't think people should take everything for granted. You all just want and want and want and expect to have

ABI. Are you going to start going on about 'my generation' again because I'll leave

NAOMI. No
    Stay
    Just stay there
    Play me something
    On your phone

ABI. Yeah
    Drake

NAOMI. No
Come on
Something nice and calming

ABI *plays some music*

ABI. You like Mark don't you?

NAOMI. Course we do –

I get this weird smell off him
Like dogs who sniff other dogs and think nah fuck it –
not you
I get this prickle in my cells, it says no not him, not you,
you smug cunt
It says get away get away get away
I don't say any of this to you
I don't want to hurt you or push you away

I think he's fine

ABI. He's my fiancé

NAOMI. More than fine

SHATTERED GLASS – 3

2006, 2013 and 2023.

NAOMI *drops a glass. It shatters.* TONY *drops a glass. It shatters.* MARK *throws a glass at* ABI. *It shatters.*

MARK. **sorry – I'm sorry.**	NAOMI. **Sorry I um – broke a glass**	TONY. **Sorry I um – broke a glass**
		LIL. Tony?
	FRANK. So you stood on it	
	NAOMI. I wanted to… yes.	
ABI. my face		TONY. I can't feel **my hands**
MARK. you're bleeding		

HANDS

2020.

ABI. Hold my hand

MARK. Why

ABI. Just hold it

MARK. Your hands are bleeding from all that bloody hand-washing

ABI. Aren't your hands bleeding?

MARK. No

ABI. They're clammy but cold at the same time

MARK. bad circulation
Why we doing this

ABI. It's nice
You have such big hands

MARK. And a really big –

ABI. No… no don't, I'm being romantic
Just hold it
Never let go

MARK. You're not wearing your ring

ABI. Washing up
I was washing up

MARK. Go put your ring on

ABI. Can't we just stay here

MARK. I said now

Do you know what I'm going out
actually I can't do this –

ABI. You've already been out –
we're only allowed out once a –

Mark	**LIL.** Tony
Mark	Tony
	darling –
Don't lock the door	**Don't touch the / door**
Mark –	
	TONY. out – out –

LIL. please
Tony sit down please
Tony
I know you want to go
outside but we / can't

TONY. out out

LIL. We can't darling
It's not safe right now

TONY. oww owww now now

LIL. Tony
We can't go wandering off
Can we
We have to / stay here

TONY. The fucking door…

LIL. Because you touch
things and fall over –
And get confused

TONY. out now out now

LIL. And last time you
screamed in that woman's
face and the germs you see
people are so frightened
She started crying
And I told her
I did try and explain but
she just ran
And / Tony stop

TONY. out out now NOW

LIL. Don't hit me
   Don't hit me
   I said
   Tony
   Come on darling
   No

TONY. nnuuuuuu nuuuuuu

LIL. Tony we can go out later

He starts crying.

TONY. LET ME OUT
   LET ME OUT
   LET ME OUT
   LET MEEE OUUT

LIL. There there… there
   there…

I DON'T LIKE HER HEARING

2000.

FRANK. What's wrong?

NAOMI. I, maybe we could

FRANK. What?

NAOMI. I don't like her hearing

FRANK. She's asleep

NAOMI. No I can hear her, she's not

FRANK. She is, she's asleep

NAOMI. I just think –

FRANK. She doesn't know what's going on though does she, jesus

NAOMI. Yeah but I
Please maybe can we just, I'll just – please

> FRANK *and* NAOMI *have sex,* NAOMI *keeps her eyes shut, she doesn't make a noise.* FRANK *comes.*
> ABI *cries.*

EXPLAIN IT TO ME

2016.

MARK. Why

ABI. Because you love it and it makes no sense to me
   It's just a pile of words
   Mechanical engineering, like I say it and I see… what I think a motor, what does a motor actually look like?
   I don't even drive
   I mean what – what do you do all day
   Every day
   Is it like planes and trains or
   Is it
   How things work or
   Space?
   Is that it – is it space and like energy and rockets and physics and shit
   What is it, what actually is it
   Because I do media right, I do media and that means sort of nothing and everything and I don't really care – like I've never cared
   My parents wanted me so badly to care about something like ice-skating or piano lessons or dance or bike-riding or fuck like every single thing they could try over and over – and I just don't really care about shit.
   I don't
   It's like this massive internal failing in me, that secretly Mark I don't really care –
   Like there's this hole in me, or my soul, where art or music should be or like I dunno fucking friends or TV shows or musicals right – but it's not
   And I like my mates, but I never really like had many
   To be honest
   And I just thought – yeah
   And I never knew really what my dad did, does, like meetings and briefcase right and long days and missing holidays and being a bit of a cunt when he was stressed, and my mum gave up work when she had me

Like some sort of old-fashioned like housewife person
And I'm an only child so really like what was she doing right – what was she actually doing all day every day
Apart from like Halloween costumes and shit like that
World Book Day.
I mean looked amazing but like come on
I don't think I knew how to be interested.
Is it natural or
So how does it feel for you when you – like when you found this really intense specific thing
Please

MARK. It's like... it's like cars and planes and shit
And forces and yeah vibrations
And how much stress and tension can something take
It's about static objects and moving objects, or moving objects in a moving object, it's fucking heat and combustion and yeah motors and circuits and the flow of steam or energy or current
It's bridges and aerodynamics
It's air-con in the fucking library.

It's... it's how we interact and shit...
So yeah
Yeah it's cool

ABI. I really fancy you right now

MARK. Do you know what I want
I want like five kids

ABI. Five fuck off

MARK. Yeah five go on
And like this house – with a projector on the ceiling one of them
You seen them
And you all sit on this massive sofa
With your popcorn machine and you just watch like all the films on there
Something for the kids

ABI. *Paddington*

MARK. Great film

ABI. One of the best

MARK. And then something for the grown-ups

ABI. *Paddington 2*

MARK. Very fair enough
And we have like those massive fucking wine glasses

ABI. Yes and we know about wines

MARK. Yes

ABI. And like a separate fridge for the wines
Prosecco on tap – a beer subscription

MARK. IPA
We have that massive barbecue thing that people have

ABI. Yessss on a deck with like fucking fairy lights and bunting

MARK. Yeah and a hot tub

ABI. Naff
But yes
And one of those beds that is half the room

MARK. And a bath like a one of them nice stand-alone baths

ABI. Ooh sexy

MARK. Yeah and a power shower

ABI. Shower room

MARK. Fuckkkkkkk shower room

ABI. And a balcony – cute
And what else

MARK. Just everything
Garage
A shed

ABI. Ha

MARK. Yeah a garden shed

ABI. For what

MARK. Like stuff
All the paddling pools and toys and ooh get them one of those little mini-cars

ABI. No no way

MARK. Yeah

ABI. They're stupid

MARK. They're amazing
For the five kids

ABI. Do they each have one?

MARK. Yeah Lamborghini, Porsche, Mercedes, whole range

ABI. Ha fleet of cars

MARK. Make them drive us around in them

ABI. Make them race each other

MARK. Winner gets to choose which Deliveroo

ABI. Spoilt

MARK. They're going to be so spoilt
I'm going to spoil them
We're going to be so happy

ABI. Yeah…

LITTLE SIPS

2020.

LIL. The air is better you can taste it
   It's… it's cleaner
   And the birds are louder
   There's this pressure behind my eyes
   And sometimes it hurts so hard I forget to breathe

   And if I'm honest, if I'm really truly honest, like proper honest I wish, I wish for all my love of you, for all my bundled love of you, my deep proper love of you. I hadn't married you because this wasn't supposed to be it. I'm sorry. But that's – that's… that's the truth. We weren't supposed to be this.

TONY. *I'm… s… s… s… sorry. I am.*
Hold my hand
Pl… please

LIL *holds his hand.*

LIL. There, there small sips, and swallow that and there we go. Good boy, good boy.

TONY. *Please I –*

LIL. Shush now, shhh

   There there let go – go on, you let go.

   TONY *dies.*

   Oh
   Oh my heart.

I'VE MET SOMEONE

2015.

ABI. I've met someone

NAOMI. Oh
　That's nice – that's so great Abi

ABI. Yeah
　He's great

NAOMI. That's great, I'm really pleased

ABI. He's the year above

NAOMI. Ooh that's good

ABI. Yeah
　He's doing mechanical engineering

NAOMI. Oh wow – handsome *and* clever

ABI. Yeah
　Which is pretty intense actually
　So I'm thinking of leaving

NAOMI. What?

ABI. Leaving uni

NAOMI. What

ABI. I just think it's not for me

NAOMI. Abi are you –

ABI. Joking – no
　Yes
　Psych

NAOMI. silly Abi
　And are you… are you being careful Abi?

ABI. What

NAOMI. At night

ABI. What do you mean?

NAOMI. Drinking and stuff – uni it's very
People get taken advantage – people attack people, put things in drinks, boys fight, girls wear silly things – are you using protection

ABI. Oh my god what have you been watching

NAOMI. *Panorama*

ABI. Knew it

NAOMI. You sound happy

ABI. I am happy
He makes me really happy

NAOMI. And what about friends, and your course

ABI. Fine

NAOMI. Just fine, say more than that

ABI. Mark says you unmake all those mates anyway in your second year so what's the point

NAOMI. Oh okay
And do you go to clubs or

ABI. No they're shit
Mark says it's all about house parties

NAOMI. Right – and what about the parties then –

ABI. Nah we don't usually bother. Mark says they're a bit boring really.
Oh Mark's here –
Gotta go Mum byeeeeee.

LIST

TONY. Armchair

    laptop

 table

   glass

ice

ice – um skates

up... stairs

   light

kitchen

      fridge

hoo... hoo... hoover

   carpet

window

     ow... ow... outside

         Inside

    hair... hair... hairbrush

brush

    your hair in my soup
    hoo... hoo... hoover
  my hand on your knee
thigh... thigh... thigh bone

         skilled

  Scullet

       Misc

         fish

    supper

                        slipper

face

                your face
                I r... r... remember
                            shop... sign... fell
    out the – face
                                fall...
                        Happy anniversary
                        I love you
                        I can sssay it, I will always
                        sayyy it

    I no words
    No words I don't need words
    Say, say, say, say it

                        Hello

                                Hello

                                        Helloo

    My voice
    This is my voice

                    Stars explode in the sky
                    I see the ones that rain
                    Bright lights

                                Even brighter
                                So bright

I'm hot now nowwww

                Get, get get away, get away

                                Your hand on my thigh
                                I pull you in closer

    I   hold you
                            Hold me
            Hold my my my hand
    My hand

I hold your hand so tight it bursts

                        Pull you so close I could kiss you
        Eat you
I sleep next to you

                        Touch, chhh chhhhh the
                        flesh of you

        Hold you
        Cold now
        Dead fish
                I'm
                        I'm, I'm I'm   I'm
I

                        Can we stop now?

SHED – 5

2024.

FRANK. Naomi.
    I don't understand what you're doing –
    Look, I was never very good at talking about – well about anything and
    That wasn't my thing
    I sometimes think about what happened –
    I do
    I know I don't talk about it, but that's because well words are a bit
    Even that's a cliché
    I have a lot of anger about everything really – everything we've created makes me want to choke myself, hard. I find it hard to breathe sometimes, to physically open my mouth and let the air in.

    You have to stop this
    Naomi you have to stop now –

    I'm going to go and make us that lasagne…
    Do you want some
    Naomi
    LOOK AT ME

HIT ME BABY ONE MORE TIME

2005.

They do the routine.

NAOMI/ABI. HIT ME BABY ONE MORE TIME – URGH

ONE OF THOSE DAYS

2020.

LIL. Funeral over Zoom
   That's not really a
   That just doesn't count
   They came
   Well their floating heads popped up
   Tweedledum and Tweedledee and I smiled thinking of you saying that and then realised that I was smiling on camera
   At one point I thought should I put something in the chat
   The chat box
   Should I just press leave
   How is this happening?
   I only bothered wearing a black top
   Because that's all anyone could see
   I hope you don't mind

   I got a food delivery in special
   Sticky prawns
   The shells are stuck in my fingernails
   No one to lick them out
   No one to make that joke about the prawns to
   Not even able to go to a shit pub and have a warm wine and eat a tiny sandwich whilst people come and shake your hand and feel seen
   But that's how it is I suppose
   It's so quiet all the time
   The birds are really fucking loud and it's
   It's like
   I would like to think of a way to kill myself but there's no... there's no... easy way
   Someone sent me a voucher for a sound bath
   But the company have gone online
   And I just
   I just
   Can't really be bothered to breathe today
   Maybe I'm glad you can't see this
   You were already so confused

Time is losing meaning for all of us
I swear it was only a year but it's been more
More than that
Hasn't it.
You deserved so much more

I might have to get a dog or something, cat maybe.
Fucking ridiculous
Can you imagine
You always lied and said you were allergic
I know you weren't
I don't like animals much
First husband had a massive dog that he would use to scare me
Go in there or he'll bite yer
He did once, on the bum
Had to get a tetanus shot
I never really told you about him. Did I?
I killed him
He's buried in the walls.
I cut him into pieces and made him into soup, and poured him down the drains
I castrated him and burnt his eyes out with the poker we use to stoke the fire
I pulled all his teeth out and fed him to the dog
I tied him to the radiator till his flesh sizzled

I didn't

Not really

I just ran away
Lucky there was somewhere to go back then.

He met someone else and eventually

He went to prison

Because he killed her

I've always felt guilty about that.

HONEYMOON

Lights up. 2024.

MARK. Suncream?

ABI. Got some in the –

LIL. Did you see them?

MARK. Fuck it's hot in here

ABI. Air-con just over by the

She's a bit much
You would say she was
already tangoed before
she's even been on holiday,
and I would say – it's
called fake tan you old sod

MARK. Come here

Can't believe this place

Can't believe we've managed this. I swore he was going to check my bag and find you – arrest me for drugs.

She has taken a ziplock bag of his ashes out of the suitcase.

ABI. That swimming pool

What's worse, dead husband or a gram of coke?

Did you see their faces when I went out in my bikini earlier – someone my age daring to go in the swimming pool, I think she nearly retched

MARK. **Does it hurt**	**Does it hurt?** My heart?
ABI. **All the time**	**All the time**
MARK. Here – some ice	
	Thirty years
ABI. **Did you ever think…**	**Did you ever think**
MARK. What?	
ABI. That **we would end up married, like this** **I never knew I would find this**	**we would end up like this** **I never knew I would find this**
The wedding was nice.	
MARK. It didn't rain	
ABI. Can we just lie next to each other in bed…	…Wish you were lying next to me in bed.
MARK. Bit of a waste Waste of money on the holiday It's our honeymoon	
ABI. I know	
	Hold on – I think I can hear her – is she crying?
MARK. Are you crying?	
	Surely not
ABI. **No…**	**No** Maybe I should
MARK. For fuck's sake.	
…	

LIL. Perfect place for it isn't it?

ABI. Sorry

LIL. Are you on your honeymoon?

ABI. Sorry, I –

LIL. You on your honeymoon – the ring I noticed and you have the glow
   The honeymoon aura we call it
   We, sorry I come here a lot, before Covid, and there's always honeymooners
   It's where we came – my late husband and I

ABI. Yes
   Oh yeah
   Yeah

LIL. Lovely isn't it

ABI. Hmm

LIL. What room you in?

ABI. Sorry

LIL. One of the ones with the view?

ABI. Yeah

LIL. Yes us too

ABI. Okay

LIL. It's nice and quiet isn't it?
   Actually stress-free

ABI. Yeah

LIL. Your face – that looks nasty

ABI. An old cut – won't heal – keeps getting infected, I pick the scabs, the pus…

LIL. Sea water sort that out

ABI. Yeah

LIL. Though you've not got your swimmers on

ABI. No. I didn't want to

LIL. Here he is
This yours?

MARK. Yeah
I'm getting a drink

LIL. I was just asking about your wedding

MARK. Yeah?

LIL. It sounds like it was lovely

MARK. Yeah it was good

ABI. He got so drunk he passed out and missed the dancing
We had to get a room in the hotel
We were meant to be flying that night

LIL. Boys will be boys eh

MARK. Want anything –

ABI. No thanks babe

MARK. Have a drink
You in a mood

ABI. No, I'll have a Coke

MARK. Alcoholic drink
Jeezus this one eh

ABI. A beer

MARK. Shots all round
Would you?

LIL. No thank you
...

It's perfect here isn't it

ABI. Yes.
Good food

LIL. Yes – classic, unfussy
  Really lovely
  So very very lovely

  Don't cry yet – he can still see you.

  There, there

  There, there

  Feel the sand instead
  Go on really feel it in between your toes
  Sand turns to glass
  Feel the sharp prick of that sand between your feet and run

  Take it from me –

  Run.

...

ABI *packs a suitcase.*

MARK. What the fuck do you think you're doing –

ABI. Just leave the room Mark.
  Just go downstairs sit in the bar and get a drink

MARK. Are you leaving – seriously –

ABI. I said go downstairs and get a drink and leave this
  Just leave this now

  MARK *moves towards* ABI. *An aeroplane takes off. Blackout.*

FORK

NAOMI. There was a fork in her face
    An actual fork
    He dug a fork into her face
    A fork stood on end in her cheek
    A fork
    He stabbed the meat of her face with a fork and for a
    moment it stood there, stood out
    It reverberated
    A fork

SHED 6 / CACOPHONY

2024.

NAOMI *is very nearly finished building the shed.*

FRANK. I couldn't look anyone in the eye today
they all kept lining up to shake my hand
and I kept counting shoes
Naomi
LOOK AT ME
I want her back, I want her back too
This isn't just about you
Was I a good dad – was I?
Naomi –
For Christ's sake
Say something
It's getting cold
Your hands are bleeding
Please Naomi.
I need you to come inside now

It's nearly midnight
I think we should all go inside now –
how about that Naomi,
let's just
rest for a bit eh, and just maybe.
…maybe just – stop.
Please can we just
Stop

ABI. Mum
    Mum

ABI. Mum… Mum… Mum… Mum… (*Continues.*)

TONY. Armchair
    Laptop
    Table

MARK. Are you?
No but are you seriously going to shut the fuck up (*Continues.*)

LIL. We stood in a park in Hackney and we watched them buckle, great big slabs of concrete just buckle asunder till the dust cloud was so big it reached up to meet it and you couldn't even see if it was, if it was even falling any more. And I couldn't stop thinking about the woman who was left in the lift when the builders shut it off – in Japan. She suffocated eventually or starved. It took ages apparently. It took a really long time.

ABI. Mum… **Mum**… **Mum**… (*Continues.*)

MARK. just shut the fuck up, for once in your fucking life, going to just stop, stop the argument stop it dead, because it's over it's actually over and fuck off I can see your lips moving, your brain thinking – you are going to open your fucking mouth and say something aren't you – you're actually going to fucking say

TONY (*continued*).
Glass
Table
Upstairs
Light
Kitchen
Fridge
Hoover
Carpet
Window
Outside
Inside
Hair
Brush
Brush
Fish
Slipper
Hair
Brush
Brush
hand
knee
Thigh
Skilled
Skullet
Misc
Fish
Slip
Sup
Hold
face
You
Me
secret

LIL. She stood in a park in her and she watched her buckle, great big slabs of her concrete just buckle asunder till she dust her was so big it reached up to meet her and you couldn't see if she was, if she was even falling her.

And I couldn't stop thinking about her she who was left in her she when the builders shut it her in Japan. She suffocated her, or starved. It took ages apparently. She took a really her she.

And she her stop thinking she that her which she her in the her when the she shut her off in her. she suffocated her, her starved. she her ages apparently. she her a really she her. And she her stop thinking she that her which she her in the her when the she shut her off in her. she suffocated her, her starved. she her ages apparently. she her a really she her.

shop Sign top saw face Happy love hair soup	She her in a her in she and her watched she buckle, her big she of her concrete just her asunder her till she her cloud was she her it reached she to her her and she couldn't her if she her, if she her even she her.

MARK (*continued*). something. Just don't, just don't, just fucking don't. Jesus. No wonder I hate you so fucking much you absolute piece of fucking shit in my life. My life is so shit. My life is so fucking shit
just shut the fuck up, for once in your fucking life, going to just stop, stop the argument stop it dead, because it's over it's actually over and fuck off I can see your lips moving, your brain thinking – you are going to open your fucking mouth and say something aren't you – you're actually going to fucking say something. Just don't, just don't, just fucking don't. Jesus. No wonder I hate you so fucking much you absolute piece of fucking shit in my life. My life is so shit. My life is so fucking shit

ABI. Mum… MUM… MUM… MUM

NAOMI. STOP!

AFTERMATH

2024.

NAOMI. I remember the first time I felt your fist in my throat, the pounding of your foot on my ribs, your tiny kicks and fluid flips, you dipped and dived, heartburn and cramps, nausea for days, I would walk into rooms and men would open doors and be police and nice and their smiles would be genuine and not tinged with malice for once. And then you came in a flurry of water and painkillers and blood and placenta and floppy-faced frog creature, lying there on my bare chest, congealed mat of hair and I see nothing but these goblin hands. So fragile, pale-blue and we are all laughing and crying and shock, maybe some shock and then you're ours. And we are told to keep you safe, so safe, so safe so I flinch with every cough, I cry with every cry you make and no sleep and my little world getting smaller, little person crawling, learning walking, the world already imploding I try and keep you, us, all safe, safe and sound, and insular this bubble of my love, my love will surely protect you from childhood cancers, and road traffic accidents and choking and cot death and colic and croup and I just want you to be safe, keep repeating safe over and over, and I want you to be happy and popular, to have friends, and be clever, to be pretty, yes I'm sorry I wanted you to be pretty and cared for and loved, to see you smile every day and keep the wolves at bay, and then you grow and the world keeps hurtling and hurting and no one seems to want to hold my hand any more. No one wants to hold my hand to cross the road. And no one seems to listen when I open my mouth, and no one seems to see me any more, maybe they never did. But they see you – they all see you and they look and they stare and it's as if they smell the freshness, and I can't say or do anything right, and the world keeps burning and spinning and hurting and we tut and we watch as towers fall and countries burn and men destroy the very air we breathe and the water is poison but you're a grown-up now, you'll be okay, I can only do so much, I did well, I'm here for you, every argument, every recipe, every broken light bulb. I am here for you with

comfort and answers, and I think you're safe now someone
to walk her home at night, someone to go to the party with –
no need to even go to the party, she's safe now. Not one of
them, not that poor girl walking home alone at night, not her,
not that one, she's safe inside with him, with that man, that
nice man who made her smile, that not-so-nice man that
didn't always make her smile. That man, that man
That man who loved her fiercely, we say fiercely, we are told
he loved you fiercely, I loved you fiercely, I love you fiercely –
And I can see it – my – your life spread out in front of me like
a cloth, every wine stain, and every crumb and the bumps in
the road are so clear and so fine – and there it is – there it is,
all of it all at once, and me at the centre, a centrepiece of my
blood and womb and I'm bleeding, keep bleeding, dying –
you're lying there and dying and we didn't even know it. And
now you're – where are you, where are you Abi.
And I see every time he hurt you, pierced your skin, every
concerned call, voicemail, forgotten date, missed email, tone,
bruise, mark, finger, fork, knife, strangle, chokehold, bite,
burn, cigarette, iron, poker, blade, smash, grab and guts and
go. It's a drip, a drip, a deluge, a flood, a charge, an electric
shield, a force field, a supernova, a nuclear war, a terrorist
attack, a detonation, a fist and a punch and a scream and
a don't wake the neighbours and a night out and a what was
that and a go back to bed, and don't worry about it, and
a you should be careful about that kind of behaviour, and
a drink and a drink and a drink and a bang bang bang bang
bang bang bang.
and I should've should've should've could I
Stop this. Can we, is there any – how would we
Who stops this
Why does this
Where are you – where are you Abi
Abi
I would kill them if I could Abi, I would kill them all I want
to tear and beat and burn the tablecloth. I will supernova this
world, explode and rain down upon them all I will tear this
fucking world to pieces and start again –
I think you want the same – don't you? Don't you?

                                             ...Ten
                                             Nine
                                             Eight
                                             Seven
                                             Six
                                             Five
                                             Four

FRANK. I knew she'd said something

NAOMI. Of course she did – do you want another? I've hidden some – behind the sofa. I love New Year –

FRANK. Really?

NAOMI. No, I just, I like the fireworks, I really love a firework – the explosion in the sky, the ones that rain –

FRANK. I want this year gone to be honest – bring on 1994

NAOMI. It's been alright actually, I got a / job

FRANK. Will you kiss me at New Year – when the clock strikes will you?

                                             Three
                                             Two
                                             One

EXPLOSION

2024.

NAOMI *explodes the shed.*

ABI. Mum? Can you see me?

LIL. Take it from me – run.

NAOMI. Yes – oh my heart yes.

> *Older* NAOMI *lights a firework – she watches it glow, she holds* ABI's *hand until* ABI *slips away with* TONY. FRANK *dances with* MARK *as* LIL *scatters Tony's ashes on a beach. Younger* NAOMI *takes off her heels and runs and runs and runs and runs out of the theatre and through the streets.*

> *The tablecloth is wiped clean. Time rewrites itself. None of it ever happened.*

> *A shed sits on a stage.*

> *End.*

ADDITIONAL SCENES

WOOF

2001.

ABI. Hold my hand
   Mummy
   Hold it
   No don't go

NAOMI. But Mummy needs to have her dinner booboo, it's late

ABI. No

NAOMI. Okay

ABI. Lie down

NAOMI. Right just for a bit

ABI. Like a dog

NAOMI. No

ABI. Yes

NAOMI. Okay

ABI. Just lie there
   And speak to me
   And don't leave

NAOMI. For a bit

ABI. yes
   Like a dog though
   Bark

NAOMI. No darling – that's not what mummies do

ABI. Mummies do what I tell them to.

NAOMI. No, no – bedtime now Abi
   Sleepy time

ABI. Woof just a little bit
   …

NAOMI. No

ABI. Yes – woof

NAOMI. Woof

COMPROMISE

2021.

NAOMI. And how are you – any news?

ABI. Yeah… fine…
   I don't know
   I feel a bit
   Funny
   About stuff
   About um
   Mark
   Relationships

   They're hard

NAOMI. I know, Abi but you have to work at them –
   They take time, work, effort
   Have you upset him?

ABI. no – why is it always my fault?!

NAOMI. Well darling you're tough, you know that, you can be tough to –

ABI. I'm not tough to live with Jesus

NAOMI. No but you know, you can be a bit quick to you know
   You know

ABI. I don't know

NAOMI. But it's all okay? Have you been arguing – you should never go to bed on an argument

ABI. You and Dad argue all the fucking time

NAOMI. Yes but we always make up
   Choose your battles that's what I say

ABI. Yeah but it's… it like… he sometimes, like our arguments can be… they can be
   Really bad

NAOMI. And that's why you have to communicate.
   And say sorry
   Men hate saying sorry – so sometimes you just have to take one for the team

Better to just get it over with you know
Then you can move on

ABI. Yeah... no it's just he can be

NAOMI. All men are sulkers Abi

ABI. Yeah, yeah he's just a bit – angry sometimes

NAOMI. They're all angry – they don't have friends like women do
That's why – you just have to make him dinner and try and treat him a bit
Tell him you care

ABI. I do care!
What about he makes me dinner –

NAOMI. Yes. But it's about well compromise isn't it
But not too much obviously but not being too proud either
And I suppose it's just about sharing the load really

ABI. Yeah

NAOMI. So it's going to be fine
All couples have bumps
It's just what happens
Part of being a grown-up sweetheart
It'll get better I promise

ABI. Yeah it's just it's been so up and down and sometimes I think –
Is this okay...
Like is he

NAOMI. It's just a phase, every couple has them – you've been through so much together.
He's a nice man Abi, one of the good ones.

ABI. Yeah
Yeah... I better go Mum

NAOMI. See you next Sunday for cousin Charlotte's thing

ABI. Yeah

NAOMI. She's put on so much weight

ABI. Bye Mum...

WHAT'S THAT SONG/WORD?

2007.

NAOMI. One banana, two banana, three banana four

ABI. Na-na-na-na-na-na-na-na-na
Dooo doo doo dooo do doo doo

NAOMI/ABI. La la la la la la la

FRANK. What song is that?

    TONY. What word is that… that word…

They sing it again. They laugh.

You're ganging up on me

    Banana… Christ.

ABI. Silly Daddy   LIL. Silly man.

STOP TAKING THE PILL

1995.

NAOMI. We've been having sex quite a lot, that's a good thing,
I think a positive step
A good thing

Sometimes it hurts but I don't think that's you, I think maybe
that's me, I think maybe something's just going on down,
a bit wrong, maybe just like a thing...
We should keep trying though, we should try again, like
I could stop taking the pill and we could, because I think that
would be something, yes I would be good at that I think.

LIST

1997.

NAOMI. *The washing, the ironing,*
the cleaning, the scrubbing, the dishwasher,
the putting away, the hoovering,
the making the bed, the changing the sheets,
the post office, the broken phone, the customer service,
the internet, the bills, the shopping, the putting away,
the texting, the birthday cards, the Christmas cards,
the presents, the dinner, the breakfast,
the lunchtime, the packed lunch, the dinner party,
the alcohol, the bin bags, the recycling, the food bin,
the other bin, the garden waste, the gardening,
the fixing, light bulbs, the radiators,
the holiday booking, the barbecue,
the fridge, the washing the bin out,
the hoover bags, the dry-cleaning,
the winter wardrobe, the spring clean,
the autumn leaves, the gutter, the antihistamines,
the paracetamol, the optician's, the doctor's appointment,
the hospital appointment, the mammogram,
the smear test, the inoculations, the mmr,
the jab, the flu vaccine, the tea, the coffee,
the milk, the hand sanitiser, the Tube, the bus,
the car, the MOT, the UTI, the insurance,
the life insurance, the house insurance,
the mortgage, the bank, the business loan,
the credit card, the charity, the food bank,
the parking, the lessons, the drop-off,
the pick-up, the school assembly, the parents' evening,
the friends, the dinner, the drinks, the cinema,
the Christmas tree, the decorations, the string,
the pictures, the parties, the rug, the windows,
the gutter, the drains, the bathroom, the sink,
the washing machine, the drying, the hanging, the –

2001 – TERRORISM

NAOMI. Oh god, oh god it's
  terrible
  Those poor people
  This is
  Fuck
  Oh god   LIL. **Oh god**
  Frank

  Frank come watch this

FRANK. Christ

                                     TONY. Is this real?

NAOMI. It's real, I can't
  believe this is real

  Do you not see this!
  There are people jumping
  Frank

FRANK. I can see that Naomi
  I'm watching the same
  fucking thing here

                                     TONY. Fuck

                                     LIL. …I can't look

KNIFE

1997.

NAOMI, *pregnant,* FRANK *stands pointing a knife at her belly.*

NAOMI. That's not funny

FRANK. It's hilarious

WHAT YEAR IS IT?

(?)

TONY. Where've you been?

LIL. What – I told you, there was the choir thing after work

TONY. You're lying to me

LIL. Tony –
Are you okay – you look... tired

TONY. You're a liar
I can see – what you're doing
I can see it – it's all in here –

LIL. Tony – what do you mean, you're being a bit odd darling –

TONY. I saw the messages, I saw it in the – the – the – phone
You're keeping them from me

LIL. Tony – you're worrying me now

TONY. You're a cheating bitch
A lying cheating bitch
Why would you do this to me – how could you do this to me –

LIL. Tony – I just told you I was at choir, you said yourself you were going to come along, I don't know why you're saying this –
Shit – the oven –
Tony did you –
Why's the dinner in here like this –
You could've set the house – on
I...
Tony...

TONY. Hmm...

LIL. What's the date today?

TONY. November... third of November – don't change the bloody subject...

LIL. What year

TONY. Hmm

LIL. What year Tony

What year is it?

Tony…

What year…

2005 – TERRORISM

NAOMI. Oh my god, oh my god, are you serious

          LIL. On the Tube

FRANK. **Jesus –**   TONY. **Jesus**

NAOMI. I would hate to be them right now

          LIL. How scary to be one of them right now

ABI. Mum, why are you crying, do you know them?

PERVERTS

2015.

NAOMI. Do you remember it?

              LIL. Do you?
                   Remember it?

FRANK. Of course, your uncle was a right dick

NAOMI. But it was so sunny

FRANK. Yeah, yeah it was actually – it was a lovely day

              TONY. Yeah… it was a… a… a… lovely d-d-ay

NAOMI. And that honeymoon

              LIL. the honeymoon

FRANK. Yeah that couple who clearly wanted to fuck us

              TONY. that
                  …that… um… couple, what were there… um…

NAOMI. They didn't!

FRANK. They so did.

    Perverts

             LIL. I wonder what happened to them. I hope they're okay. I know it's silly, but I kept thinking – you could be my daughter, the one I… Which is silly.

TONY AND LIL – HOUSE

1998.

LIL. This one – I can smell it

TONY. What does it smell of?

LIL. Home
Like baking and bacon or something

TONY. Maybe there's a café nearby

LIL. No it's our smell, our 'this is it' smell – a smell of fucking this one – 'buy this one' smell.

TONY. It's not even ours

LIL. Yet
Trust me – it's mine
I know it

TONY. You're being soppy today – it's a bit weird.

LIL. I'm just a bit – I dunno – excited. Feel like I'm slipping into something

TONY. It's called midlife crisis

LIL. Fuck off
It's called new beginnings

TONY. God you're good

LIL. At what?

TONY. Just making me happy

LIL. There's a second bedroom look

TONY. What use is that?

LIL. Study
Maybe –
Or you know for our separate beds when we no longer want to be near one another.
When our skin can't bear to brush up against each other and we feel repulsed by the slightest touch –
And I snore and fart you to boredom

TONY. I can't wait.

YOU HATE YOUR MUM

2016.

MARK. You fucking hate
  your mum

                                          FRANK. You fucking hate
  them

ABI. **I don't**
  That's not –
                                  NAOMI. **I don't**
  That's not

MARK. **You do**
  You fucking hate her
  Everything she says you
  flinch
                            FRANK. **You do**
  You fucking hate her

ABI. I don't

MARK. **Your eyes go hard**
  Your nose wrinkles
  You come back home
  and you fuck me nastily
                            Your eyes go hard
  Your nose –

ABI. We don't
                                  NAOMI. I don't

MARK. Every time
  Because you're angry

ABI. I'm not

MARK. **You're a bad**
  fucking liar.
                            FRANK. **You're a bad**
  fucking liar.

TERRORISM – 2017

LIL. Oh god no

FRANK. **Look –**

MARK. **Look** at this – look

NAOMI. where's that?

FRANK. London Bridge

ABI. Fuck in Manchester!

MARK. shit –

No, those poor people.

NAOMI. That's awful

That's fucked up

why can't they put it out.
I don't understand.
The whole building –
Tony – Tony oh god –

ABI. I need to call Mum –

I'll call Abi –

Abi, Abi?

…Mum?

A Nick Hern Book

Shed: Exploded View first published in Great Britain in 2024 as a paperback original by Nick Hern Books Limited, The Glasshouse, 49a Goldhawk Road, London W12 8QP, in association with the Royal Exchange Theatre, Manchester

Shed: Exploded View copyright © 2024 Phoebe Eclair-Powell

Phoebe Eclair-Powell has asserted her moral right to be identified as the author of this work

Cover photography by Felicity McCabe

Designed and typeset by Nick Hern Books, London
Printed in the UK by Mimeo Ltd, Huntingdon, Cambridgeshire PE29 6XX

A CIP catalogue record for this book is available from the British Library

ISBN 978 1 83904 274 4

CAUTION All rights whatsoever in this play are strictly reserved. Requests to reproduce the texts in whole or in part should be addressed to the publisher.

Amateur Performing Rights Applications for performance, including readings and excerpts, by amateurs in English should be addressed to the Performing Rights Manager, Nick Hern Books, The Glasshouse, 49a Goldhawk Road, London W12 8QP, *tel* +44 (0)20 8749 4953, *email* rights@nickhernbooks.co.uk, except as follows:

Australia: ORiGiN Theatrical, *email* enquiries@originmusic.com.au, *web* www.origintheatrical.com.au

New Zealand: Play Bureau, 20 Rua Street, Mangapapa, Gisborne, 4010, *tel* +64 21 258 3998, *email* info@playbureau.com

United States of America and Canada: Independent Talent Group, see details below

Professional Performing Rights Applications for performance by professionals in any medium and in any language throughout the world (and amateur and stock performances in the United States of America and Canada) should be addressed to Independent Talent Group Ltd, 40 Whitfield Street, London W1T 2RH, *tel* +44 (0)20 7636 6565

No performance of any kind may be given unless a licence has been obtained. Applications should be made before rehearsals begin. Publication of this play does not necessarily indicate its availability for amateur performance.

www.nickhernbooks.co.uk/environmental-policy

www.nickhernbooks.co.uk

facebook.com/nickhernbooks

twitter.com/nickhernbooks